I0605587

"I can offer no higher compliment than this: Someone I love dearly picked up this book during a stretch of pressing darkness, and it helped them. Thank you for making something that helps to lift the darkness. I'd like to hand this beautiful book out left and right."

Shauna Niequist, author of *I Guess I Haven't Learned That Yet*

"As someone who has wanted to end it all in her own season of depression, and who accompanies many others in theirs, *In the Low* is the gift I've longed for. Too many words, attempts to fix, and 'helpful' prayers bruise and bind souls needing support and salve. *In the Low*'s words and images lean into each other in a structure of support, reminding readers of the tender and terrible gift of being human, and point toward the One who makes all this humaning have meaning, after all. I will be reaching for this resource for years to come."

Tara Owens, executive director, Anam Cara Ministries, spiritual director, and author of *Embracing the Body*

"Depression has a way of turning prayer into a foreign language, leaving us stammering in the dark for words we once spoke with ease. *In the Low* gives voice to those struck speechless by despair, honoring the sacred truth that faith often speaks through the shadows. McRoberts and Erickson grant us permission to bring our whole selves—including our deepest pain—and lay them before the Divine. I can't recommend this book highly enough for all who need to be reminded that God meets us not despite our darkness but within it."

Jonathan Merritt, columnist and author of *Learning to Speak God from Scratch*

"*In the Low* acts as a companion to our seasons of melancholy without rushing us to 'fix' anything. It meets us where we are, as we are. This book resonates deeply within my angsty artist heart, and I'm so grateful it exists in the world."

Jess Janz, poet and founder of Dinner with Strangers

"I've heard someone describe art and poetry as 'language in service of the Unsayable.' There's nothing like finding those kinds of words in seasons when they're so often absent—let alone paired with images so capable of stoking ashes into awe. I felt seen and loved (at the same time?!) in these pages. I found words my spirit has only been able to groan (I even caught her dancing with the Low). Scott and Justin created a hand to hold in the valley, and I'm grateful to the both of them for how warm it is."

Levi The Poet, spoken word artist

"If you have experienced depression, or if you are close to someone who is in that low place right now, you know that well-meaning friends, family members, and clergy often say things that make you feel worse. As I read the honest, simple prayers in this book and let the clear and powerful illustrations do their work on me, I felt: 'This will help, not hurt. This will help make things better, not worse.' You will treasure this book, I predict, and come back to it again and again."

Brian D. McLaren, author of *Faith After Doubt* and *Life After Doom*

"*In the Low* is an accompaniment for the places inside that deserve to be known, the wordless places that need words, the dark and diffuse places that need form and shape. In being met in the Low we can come to find how these places not only are part of being human but are full of treasures."

Dr. Hillary L. McBride, psychologist, podcast host, author, and mother

"We don't need prescriptive answers; we don't need anyone to explain away the pain that can't be rationalized to begin with. We only need companions who fully see us and know us where we are, in order to get through the night. *In the Low* is that sort of wise companion—a warm, tender, desperately needed book that doesn't speak *about* the ache but from *inside of it*. This is the rare work of 'spirituality' that is not abstract, detached, clichéd, or avoidant but instead gives us the language to speak the unspeakable."

Jonathan Martin, author of *How to Survive a Shipwreck* and *The Road Away from God*

"This is not your mother's prayer book, though it did make me cry! *In the Low* is both simple and subversive, inviting us not simply into peace but fuller personhood. Inside the pages of this foxy book, Scott Erickson and Justin McRoberts have created space to be welcomed home into the wholeness that isn't actually lost on your lowest days."

K.J. Ramsey, licensed therapist and author of *The Book of Common Courage*

"This book is not a cure, nor a map to a brighter shore, but a quiet companion for the journey. In a world heavy with worry and shadowed by the ache of futility, it speaks not to fix but to witness. Its art, poetry, and prayers sit gently beside us, holding space for the weight we carry. It shines a subtle light—not to banish the dark but to illuminate it, revealing the fragile beauty in being. Here is a tender guide, not to answers but to the shared humanity of searching, waiting, and finding meaning in the in-between."

David Gungor, *The Brilliance*

"*In the Low* gives us permission to name the ache in our hearts without rushing to fix it. What a relief to discover honest prayers and art that offer a flicker of hope for the dark nights of the soul. These pages create space to stop pretending everything is fine and instead invite us to rest in the sacred mystery of a God who stays, even when we're at our lowest. I'm grateful for this book. I only wish I had it sooner."

Kayla Craig, author of *Every Season Sacred* and *To Light Their Way* and creator of Liturgies for Parents

"One of the most difficult parts of dwelling in a season of depression can be the feelings of isolation and loneliness that come with it. Through this book, Justin and Scott offer us words, images, and their own selves in ways that give us a sense of companions who see us, know us, and care. In my experience, that can make all the difference. Thank God for this offering and for these two faithful and prophetic friends."

Donna Hatasaki, senior director of spiritual formation, Young Life

"Dark seasons aren't optional—they're the price of admission for being human. When my ticket gets pulled, this is the book I'll always keep by my side. Its combination of simple words and reflective images makes it the perfect companion for navigating the Lows that inevitably find us all."

Brit Barron, author of *Should You Still Talk to Grandma?*

"If the purpose of *In the Low* was to create an honest and hopeful collection of words and images, then mission accomplished. Erickson and McRoberts have truly given us a helpful companion to carry as we slow down and sit with what life has become."

Tanner Olson, author and poet

"This book is a poignant and powerful guide through our deepest seasons of longing and grief, darkness and despair. These words and images offer a simple but stunning hope when our own prayers and imaginations fall short."

Jay and Katherine Wolf, authors of *Hope Heals*, *Suffer Strong*, and *Treasures in the Dark*

"Justin McRoberts and Scott Erickson have created a beautiful collection of word and image prayers for those of us trudging through the Low places. This work humanizes the dark seasons of life without being sentimental or prescriptive. I highly recommend this book to anyone who needs a bit of companionship through the hard work of healing and reconnection."

Stephen Roach, host of *Makers and Mystics* podcast and founder of The Breath & The Clay creative arts collective

"*In the Low* is a companion that offers the rare precision of accurately naming where you are while not leaving you by yourself. As a therapist, I'm always looking for books that combine humanity, compassion, and hope—books that will make us feel less alone. This is that book, and I will be recommending it often."

Monica DiCristina, MA, LPC, therapist and author of *Your Pain Has a Name*

"No one plans to be in the Low, but life has a way of ushering us there nonetheless. And speaking as someone who's spent time there, I know how paralyzing it can be to make decisions while in those depths. My advice? Get a copy of *In the Low* before you need it—it's precisely the kind of normalizing, affirming, and healing companion you'll be grateful to have when the Low finds you."

**Colby Martin**, author of *Unclobber* and *The Shift*

"Have you ever felt hugged by a book? If not, get ready, because this is that book. In this breathtaking volume, Scott and Justin offer us a tremendous tool that, I suspect, we'll end up using on a regular basis. Their art and words are a balm for my oft weary soul and a reminder that it's okay to not be okay. Friends, be prepared to read this book more than once."

**Nick Laparra**, podcast host of *Let's Give a Damn*

"I'm in a dark season again. So many are. Sometimes I DO need words when I have none, and I DO need images when my own screen is blank. I found the unutterable prayers of my heart in these pages. I needed a resource that is real and raw about my shadow times yet counterintuitively offers glimmers of hope rather than stealing it. Many thanks, friends!"

**Bradley Jersak, PhD**, principal of St Stephen's University

"There is nothing out there like this book. It is a must-buy. In my own seasons of Low I do not have the energy to read thousands of lofty words—I just need a hopeful image, a heartfelt thought, or words from a friend. This book gives you all three. Buy it for everyone you know because it is not if we will have a Low season but when. This book will lift you up when you need it."

**Katie Quesada**, storytelling consultant

"Any and every page of this work is a lifeline for the depth of depression and a direct line to the divine. You will find the concise brevity you need as light piercing the fog, one line and one brushstroke at a time."

**J. S. Park**, hospital chaplain and author of *As Long As You Need: Permission to Grieve*

"Sometimes a picture is worth a thousand words. Sometimes a thousand words can't express what can be said in a picture. This book, a unified gift of prayers and pictures, brilliantly strikes the heart more profoundly than a thousand books alone could do on the subject."

**Mike Donehey**, musician and author of *Grace in the Gray*

"*In the Low* offers a deeply human, prayerful companion for those seasons of inner turmoil. This book is not just a guide—it is an invitation to reconnect with the sacred conversations we are already having, often unnoticed, within ourselves. Through powerful words and images, the authors encourage us to stop striving for 'better' or 'fixed' and instead to slow down and listen deeply to the Divine presence who is always with us, even in our lowest moments."

**Pete Wilson**, life coach and author of *Plan B: What Do You Do When God Doesn't Show Up the Way You Thought He Would?*

# IN THE LOW

honest prayers for dark seasons

Justin McRoberts
& Scott Erickson

BakerBooks
a division of Baker Publishing Group
Grand Rapids, Michigan

Published by Baker Books
a division of Baker Publishing Group
Grand Rapids, Michigan
BakerBooks.com

Printed in China



Library of Congress Cataloging-in-Publication Data
Names: Erickson, Scott (Artist) author | McRoberts, Justin author.
Title: In the low : honest prayers for dark seasons / Scott Erickson and Justin McRoberts.
Description: Grand Rapids, Michigan : Baker Books, a division of Baker Publishing Group, [2025] | Includes bibliographical references.
Identifiers: LCCN 2024047305 | ISBN 9781540904256 (cloth) | ISBN 9781493447015 (ebook)
Subjects: LCSH: Anxiety—Religious aspects—Christianity | Worry—Religious aspects—Christianity.
Classification: LCC BV4908.5 .E753 2025 | DDC 152.4/6—dc23/eng/20241206
LC record available at https://lccn.loc.gov/2024047305



Cover illustration by Scott Erickson

The authors are represented by Punchline Agency, www.punchlineagency.com.

Baker Publishing Group publications use paper produced from sustainable forestry practices and postconsumer waste whenever possible.

25 26 27 28 29 30 31 7 6 5 4 3 2 1

To you, dear reader.

All of this is just noise
if not for the ongoing work
happening within you.

Thank you for the chance
to be a part of this hidden unfolding;
the quiet alchemy of your becoming.

# Before You Begin . . .

In the same way our other books are prayerful companions, this book is also a prayerful companion, one specifically designed for times and seasons of depression and anxiety.

Just as spiritual practices are less about adding things and more about removing what's in the way, prayer is not about getting God's attention but about *awakening to the voice and work of God that is already in our lives.* In our first book together, Scott and I featured a tuna can being opened by a can opener to help understand what's happening.[1]

Words and images are not prayers, themselves. Not really. They are excavation tools with which to get to the ever-present, ongoing interior conversation we are already having with the Divine. When we hear someone speak a prayer or read Scripture or sing a song that makes us say "Yes," "Amen," or even just "Hmm," what we are experiencing is the excavation tool of the words exhuming the deep prayer already within us. Words and images point to the deeper conversation that often gets lost in the noise, fear, and ego of human life. So, while our original book efforts came in response to many friends saying they struggle with prayer, we like to say that nobody is actually bad at prayer because everyone is already praying. Instead, what we can be bad at is paying attention to our insides, where prayer is already happening.

Also in our previous books, we have offered a mantra of sorts, saying "We pray because we're human, not because we're religious."

EVER-PRESENT
INTERIOR
CONVERSATION
WITH THE DIVINE

With this third tandem volume, we're adding this:

**"We spend time in the Low because we are human, not because we're broken."**

Just as we consider prayer an expression of humanity, we have experienced being Low as an aspect of that same humanity.

The work herein is deeply shaped by two other works, one of which we highly recommend and the other we will introduce to you over the course of the book. First, Johann Hari's *Lost Connections* helped us recontextualize our experience of depression and anxiety, removing it from the often frustrating, unsavory narrative in which "something is wrong with my head." Instead, Hari suggests there might be a fair bit askew in the world *around* our heads too. Without dismissing the chemical and clinical components of depression and anxiety, *Lost Connections* freed us to recognize that living with depression and anxiety is a human experience in an oftentimes inhumane world. And while the Low can be wildly complex, it is wild and complex in many of the same ways being human is always wild and complex.

Hari points at nine primary connections, without which our mental health suffers and even withers. He calls them "The Nine Causes of Depression and Anxiety":

Disconnection from Meaningful Work
Disconnection from Other People
Disconnection from Meaningful Values
Disconnection from Childhood Trauma
Disconnection from Status and Respect
Disconnection from the Natural World
Disconnection from a Hopeful or Secure Future
Disconnection due to Genes
Disconnection due to Brain Changes[2]

We were moved to create prayers in response to these categories, with the exception of Hari's chapter on causes eight and nine, focused on genes and brain changes. We feel it's more appropriate for us to point toward caring, brilliant friends who work in the clinical field, addressing these disconnections—friends like Dr. Hillary McBride and authors K.J. Ramsey and Dr. Curt Thompson. Please read and follow their work.

In the end, we organized our book into five sections rather than Hari's nine, beginning with a section entitled "Where I Am Today." We assume that if you're picking up this book, something isn't working for you where you are right now. The four other sections that follow deal with the past, our intertwined existence, the things we deeply care about, and the future or what's ahead of us.

Regardless of the order these categories appear, please approach this volume the same way we've invited you to approach the previous two.

**You do not have to read in sequential order.**

**Spend time with the prayer that is speaking the most to you.**

This is a collection of helpful words and images for the season you're in, not a sequence of pages you need to be in a hurry to finish. Our suggestion is to stop with the prayer that is excavating that deep place in you the most. Spend time with what is trying to catch your attention.

The two questions at the heart of this book are,

> "If being in the Low is part of how I exist, how do I do that?"
> "How do I live and feel whole when I am also feeling pressed down, shaken, and run over?"

And that's what makes Mary Mrozowski's Welcoming Prayer the second formative work surrounding this book.

The Welcoming Prayer, as taught by Contemplative Outreach (a community founded, in part, by Mary Mrozowski), is an embodied movement that begins with noticing sensation in one's body, welcoming what one experiences as an opportunity to consent to God's presence, and finally letting go by praying, "I let go of my desire for security, affection, and control and embrace this moment as it is."

For the purposes of this book, we're offering a simplified version of the prayer, more suitable for this book's format.[3] You'll find this prayer repeated at the beginning of each section. Think of it as an invitation to pause and ready your heart to receive what you might find in you along the way:

> *Welcome, welcome, welcome.*
> *I welcome everything that comes to me today, because I know it's for my healing.*
> *I welcome all thoughts, feelings, emotions, persons, situations, and conditions.*
> *I let go of my desire for power and control.*
> *I let go of my desire for affection, esteem, approval, and pleasure.*
> *I let go of my desire for survival and security.*
> *I let go of my desire to change any situation, condition, person or myself.*
> *I open to the love and presence of God and God's action within.*
> *Amen.*

It's important to note that at no point does the prayer ask us to welcome the hurtful circumstances, abuses, or specific acts of violence that can undo us. Instead, we are invited to welcome God's presence to and with us *in* our experiences. We are also welcoming the way our souls respond to hurtful circumstances, abuses, and violence.

We don't have to ask our souls to "keep it down" when we're suffering. We also don't have to gloss over our experiences with some kind of reasoned explanation. Instead, the Welcoming Prayer offers a way to say what is vulnerably true of us and count *that* as prayer. We also don't need to *do* something about what we've experienced. You and I get to simply be where we are, as we are, which makes the Welcoming Prayer a generous partner to this book—a book that seeks to be a companion to each of us when we've been knocked off our horse, as it were.

Speaking of being knocked off one's horse . . . (Terrible segue, I know. But go with me. It'll be worth it.)

The man we've come to call the apostle Paul saw his life as Saul undone and fundamentally changed in a flash. While I don't resonate with the speed and immediacy of his experience, I do find a significant number of parallels between Saul's moment and his short season afterward and my experiences in the Low. For one thing, while Saul was lying on the ground after falling off his horse, the people he'd been traveling with were utterly confounded.

> The men traveling with Saul stood there speechless; they heard the sound but did not see anyone. (Acts 9:7)

Been there? When people near you didn't see or hear or understand the things you were seeing and feeling (the very things that were knocking you off your horse)? I have too. And I was abundantly thankful for anyone willing to kindly companion me in that moment and through the following season. I didn't need anyone to understand or ask me to explain; I couldn't explain and I didn't understand.

Also like Saul, I needed someone to wait through my blindness and disorientation and maybe be willing to feed me when my hunger returned. I resonated with Saul living long days without the ability to accurately see the journey he was on or the steps he was taking in it. Eventually, the people who sat with Saul long enough got to share in the restoration of his sight, the recovery of his appetite, *and* the first few steps of his next season, a season in which he'd become an entirely new person with a different name.

We'd like this book to be that kind of companion for you.

Beloved, we've read the statistics about depression and anxiety and a plethora of other mental health crises. You probably have too. We don't know what to make of those statistics or how to read the upward trends. We can't make sense of it, and, to be honest, we don't really want to. Instead, because we've been there and will likely be there again, we'd rather say something like this:

Being here
In The Low
is part of
being human.

That doesn't change the fact
that being here
is hard.
We know it is.

So, while our Lows
might be
different from yours,
please know we've been there too.

And, if you'll have us,
we'd like to join you,
as friends
and prayerful companions.

# Reconnecting to **Where I Am Today**

Perhaps this Low
is simply a normal response
to the parts of life
we don't understand.

May this Low
mean a humble entrance
into parts of me and my world
I'm being invited
to know.

I'm here again.
This is taking so long.
I want to be further along.
I want to be better.

May the slowness of Your work in me
be a sign it will last.
Reassure me I am not just getting better,
I am becoming Whole.

I feel so lost.
And it is the most devastating feeling

To be lost
From You.
From me.
From everybody and everything.

Thankfully
You knew we would all come to this moment,
so you gave us the gift of Lost Stories.

The shepherd leaves the 99 to find the one lost sheep.
The woman cleans her entire house looking for the
    lost coin.
The father throws a party when the lost son
is finally returned to his seat at the family table.

I am lost.
But not to You.
I'm lost to me.
Lost to the self that doesn't work anymore.

May I see my lost-ness
not as a sign of being forgotten,
but a necessary preamble
to the celebration of my belonging.

Maybe the feeling
of giving up on myself
just means I haven't found
the Self
You invited me to be.

In this Low,
give me the Light of Grace
as I walk the dark path
toward accepting the gift
of my incarnation.

Hating myself
means living divided.
Living divided
means living lonely.

Living lonely
leaves me
in the Low.

May I grow in the capacity and desire
to embrace sadness and darkness
as aspects of my Whole Person
rather than only problems to be solved.

Teach me to be Whole.

The Teacher says
"Everyone who drinks
the water I give them
will never thirst again."

O, to be a wellspring;
to see light and life
pour over, in joy and laughter,
from the depths of my being.

For now, I will settle
for knowing I am thirsty
and receiving my thirst
as a sign I am alive.

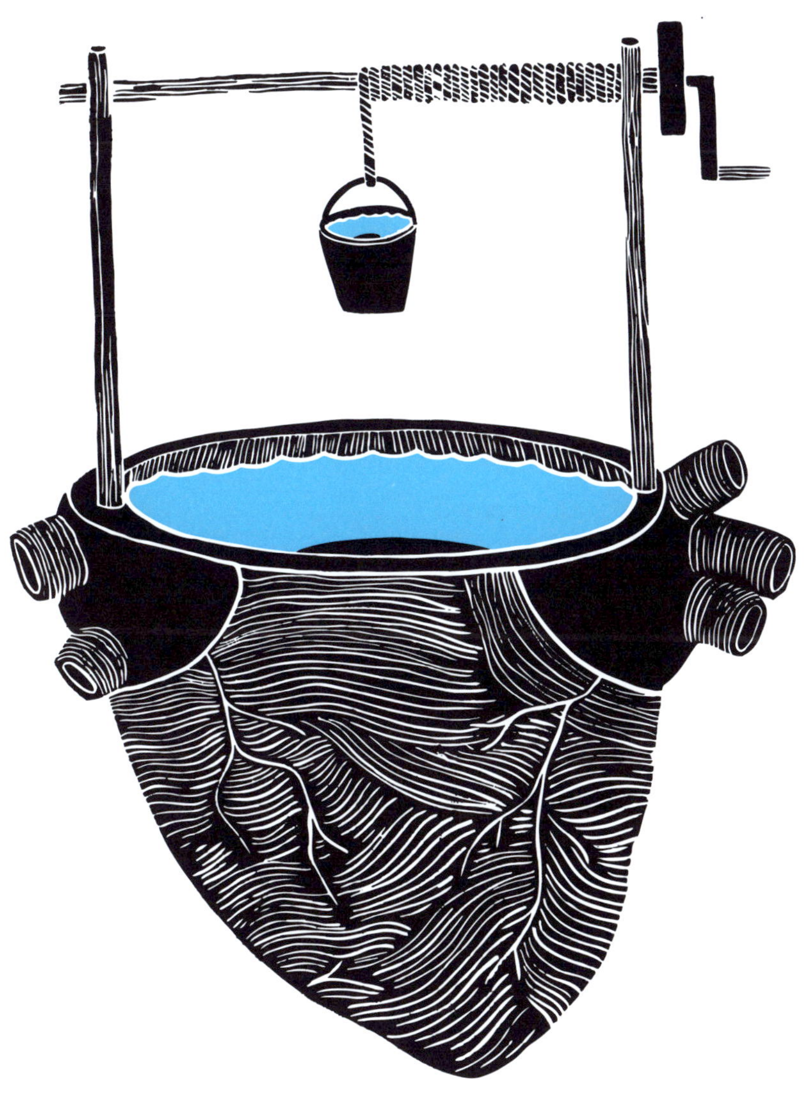

I do not want
to simply understand myself,
though there is so much
I do not understand.

Help me learn myself
with curiosity and patience,
particularly when
I do not understand what I see.

Help me learn myself
in a way that
is an investment
in the mystery of my becoming.

Help me learn myself
in a way that
transcends understanding.

Help me, in fact, to love myself.

I don't necessarily
want to be dead
I just don't want to be alive
this way
anymore.

This feels like a ridiculous prayer, but

may I be grateful
for not wanting
to be alive
this way anymore.

Let the death
of who I thought
I had to be
mean rebirth
into who
I get to be.

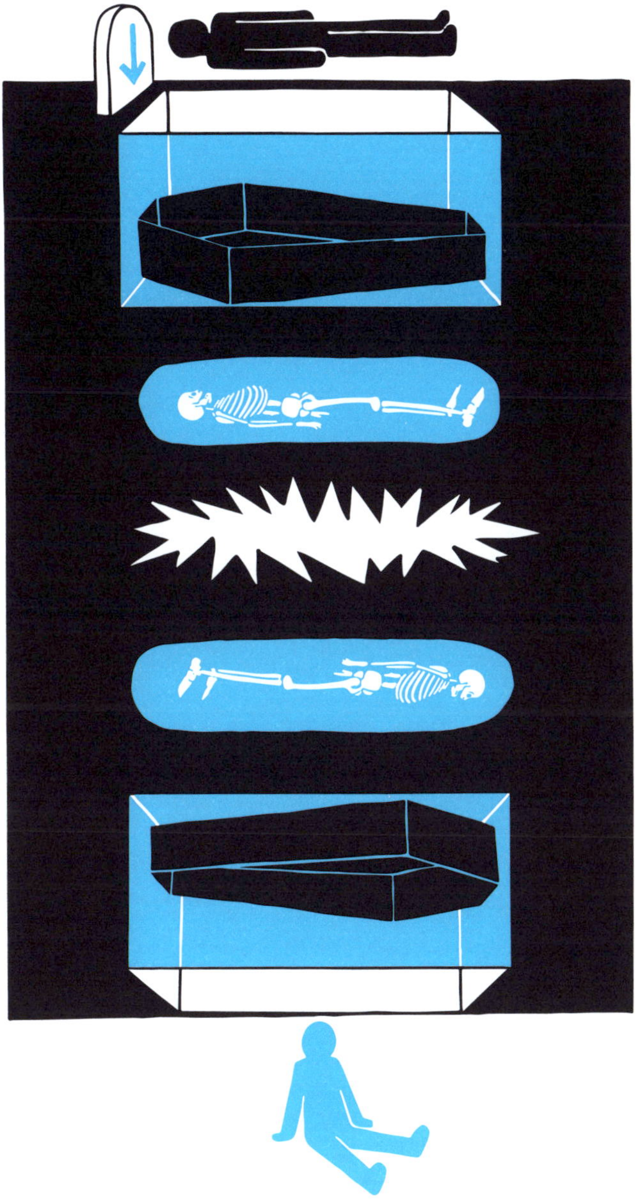

May I have
courage to believe
part of what it means
to be whole
is feeling like
I'm in pieces.

My hope is not simply
that I will rise
back to the surface
(though I do hope that).

But more than that,
my hope is
that I will learn to breathe
at this depth.

I lack the courage
of the Leper
who extended his hand
when You asked him to.

I lack the courage
to reach out
with the very parts of me
I've hidden.

Am I only healed
when I am exposed?
Is the doorway to wholeness
always shame?

Or, by some
extravagant mercy,
is there healing
in the dark places too?

Is it possible
that what you're asking of me
is to trust, here in the dark and Low,
that I am being restored?

Grant me the courage of the Leper
to extend my hand to you,
exposing things about my Self
I don't want to see.

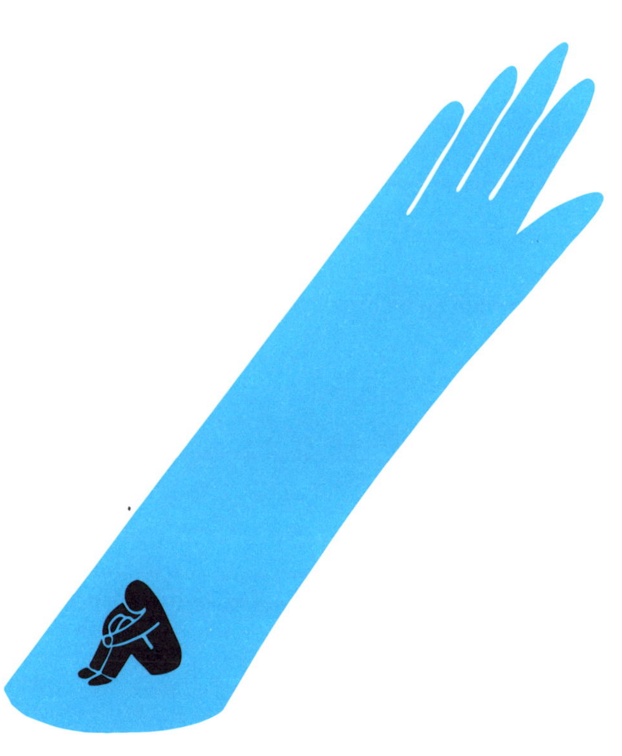

May I remember
my mind can be like
the evening sky,
more dark than light.

But the glow of the stars
makes the long nights
worth it.

Teach me
to let someone else
show me who I am
and name me
in ways I can't
(or won't).

May I see that the forces
I cannot control
are not necessarily against me.
They may very well be
the unseen and providential help
bringing me to a healed
and more whole self.

I may be lost in the woods,
but I am not the woods.

I may be lost at sea,
but I am not the sea.

I may be in the Low,
but I am not the Low.

I may be in this moment,
but I am not this moment.

May this Low
mean an unexpected excavation
to a deeper understanding
of who I am.

May I trust
that the part of me
I am missing
has gone to a place
where it can be refreshed
in order to come back to me,
anew.

May this time
separated from my whole self
not be in vain.

One thing
I do know
is that the heaviness
of this Low
makes thinkers
of us all.

Grant me the courage
to get out of my head
and not think my way
out of healing and wholeness.

# Reconnecting to
# What Happened to Me

## Considering the Disconnection from Close Relationships and Past Trauma

In the Christian tradition, resurrection and newness encompass our whole being and history, including the parts of our yesterday we'd rather leave behind. The resurrected body of Jesus was marked by the scars of his betrayal, injury, and death. So, what if those scars aren't just unfortunate reminders of a difficult season but are, instead, essential aspects of newness, wholeness, and health?

I know that's not the gospel we're sold nowadays. That gospel often sounds more like "New year, new you!" and includes the promise that the past doesn't matter anymore. But I've found that framing of what happened to me both disappointing and very distressing. First, because I am regularly aware of the injuries I'm carrying around from yesterday. And second, because I find myself frustrated when I cannot "shake it."

> So, what if I'm not supposed to shake it?
> What if the hope
> of leaving yesterday behind
> is a false and dangerous hope?
> What if
> resurrection means
> carrying my past without shame
> or embarrassment?

What if resurrection means
a newness that redeems
what happened to me
instead of ignoring it?

While I was training to be a pastor, I was told, in no uncertain terms, "You don't get to be just another person in the room. Your title changes that. So, do not expect to make a lot of friends; you will end up hurt." I hated hearing that and mentally filed the warning in the part of my mind reserved for other tall tales such as those about swimming after eating and what to do with pennies I find facedown on the sidewalk. I'd lived my early twenties with a group of people who had melded into what we called "Family," and I didn't believe for a second that anyone in my Family would hurt me. More than that, I thought it was ridiculous that wearing a title like "pastor" would change my relationship to those people.

## But/And/Then

When the floor fell out from underneath our Family, I found myself left in the lurch by folks who'd told me they'd stick by me. I found myself waiting for visits or phone calls from people I'd hoped would check on me. I found myself humiliated by things I heard said about me by people I thought had room for my shortcomings. The loss and absence of those connections ushered me into the darkest and deepest Low of my life. It was as if someone dropped a Wile E. Coyote–sized anvil through the floor of my soul's architecture and the whole house fell in.

In the half-drunken two-ish years of that Low, I learned a few things.

First, I realized there really are systems and forces working to keep me disconnected. That was what my pastoral training friend was pointing out—not that people are intrinsically awful, but that we are often unknowingly complicit in systems that work against our best interests. Every system is self-interested. Every. Single. One. And we set a terrible trap for ourselves when we ignore that truth by offering the best of ourselves to plans, schemes, and systems that are not held by the calloused, wounded hands of the betrayed and crucified Christ.

Second, I learned just how vital those loving relationships are and how hungrily my soul pursues them. When I lost the church community that I'd considered Family, I lost the ability to see myself clearly as well as the ability to recognize God. I didn't just feel lonely; I felt abandoned. Scott often says that a relationship with another human being is an invitation to see God. When those people were gone from my life, it was less of a social bummer and more of a full-blown existential crisis. I am now radically aware of the way my God connection is tied to my people connection.

More than anything else, I learned that what happened to me in the past isn't just part of my past; it's part of who I am now, and it changes how I connect with the world around me. That knowledge has reframed the way I understand woundedness. Being wounded is not just an unfortunate experience, like stepping on a piece of broken glass I might have avoided had I just been paying attention. Disappointment and injury are unavoidable and integral aspects of healthy human connection.

You and I
are going to be hurt
by other people.

You and I
are going to hurt
other people.

All of this
is part of what it means
to be whole, together.

One of the gifts of true friendship is the oddly sacred opportunity to act out of our worst selves, hurt one another, and then find out we are still loved. And not loved *despite* our dark side but loved in a way that includes the lower and lesser aspects of ourselves. We don't get to have healthy connections without hurt. We don't get to become the best, fullest "version" of ourselves without injury. We don't get new life without death.

It is entirely understandable for us to want to avoid interpersonal pain. But avoiding pain is often one of the reasons we avoid relationships in general, and that leaves us lonely.

During the Low that followed the disintegration of my church Family, I actively sought to fill the empty space in me with alcohol. But contrary to the two-dimensional narratives of film and television, I didn't drink to avoid my feelings; I drank *in order* to feel. I wanted permission to be sad and very, *very* angry. Alcohol provided a shadow of the gracious permission true friendship offers, a warm welcome to whatever was going on in me. But I'm not designed to offer my feelings and thoughts in isolation and certainly not while intoxicated. I sought the feeling of connection while avoiding the people my soul wanted to connect with. The fear of being hurt kept me from connecting, leaving me lonely. I eventually tired of emoting by myself and admitted how badly I needed other voices. Sober ones. Kind ones. Forgiving ones.

A year and a half into the hardest season I've lived thus far, I looked up long enough to notice the few folks who had stuck by me. It was a short list, Beloved, made up of people I did not expect. I'd hurt some of them. And some of them had hurt me. Yet, there we were, saying "I'm still here. I choose you." After the proverbial dust settled, the social space around me was far emptier than it had ever been. And in that emptier space, I found people who had been disappointed and injured by me *and* were willing to call me "friend." I found people who had injured me whom I sincerely wanted to reconnect with.

All of which reminded me of the warning I'd received in pastoral training, "Do not expect to make a lot of friends; you will end up hurt." What the trainer said ended up being true, in a way. I *had* been hurt. I'd also hurt people. And none of us have ever been the same. But he was wrong to suggest that *not* getting hurt was a worthy goal. The good and bad that happen between us are both part of who we are in the same way the scars on Jesus's hands, feet, sides, and back are part of who Jesus is; in fact, those scars were how his closest friends recognized him in his newness.

May it be so
with you and me
that what happened to us in the past
finds a home
in the expansive, rich soil
of our becoming.

Let's pray.

*Welcome, welcome, welcome.*
*I welcome everything that comes to me today, because I know it's for my healing.*
*I welcome all thoughts, feelings, emotions, persons, situations, and conditions.*
*I let go of my desire for power and control.*
*I let go of my desire for affection, esteem, approval, and pleasure.*
*I let go of my desire for survival and security.*
*I let go of my desire to change any situation, condition, person or myself.*
*I open to the love and presence of God and God's action within.*
*Amen.*

If I can't get out
of this situation,
may this Low
graciously give me the chance
to get underneath it.

May I receive
even this sadness
as a longing
and a hunger.

Attune my soul
to hear my own heart's whispers,
to decode the groans
and sighs of my body.

Attune my mind
so that I might know
what You have for me
here in the Low.

Depression is the smoke
from a house on fire
deep within me;
a housefire I'm becoming aware of.

Today
may I be grateful
for the trail
that is leading me
to the deeper issue

so I can deal with the problem,
extinguishing the flames
engulfing my soul.

Like water seeks
the lowest point,
my soul also
seeks the depths.

Much of who I am
exists in darkness
and at depths
I am often afraid to go.

But so much of You
exists in darkness, too.
And You have told me
darkness is as light to You.

I have also heard it said
I was woven together
in the depths.
I am starting to believe that.

Show me that
when I rest in the depths,
You are there
with me.

I have come to realize
not everyone wants me whole.
Knowing that
comes with some grief.

And yet, that grief
rescues me from the illusion
that everyone is for me
and has my best interests in mind.

May grief over the ways
I thought I was cared for
clear room in me
for thankfulness to shine on the ways I am.

Rescue me from
the illusions I live with.
They distort my soul
and keep me from truer joys.

Disillusionment clears the path
of false hope and debris
so that my heart can experience
the pain that comes with a Good Life.

Disillusionment is a way my soul tells me

"The promise of remaining unhurt
and the promise of being entirely safe
will let you down."

Remind me that a Good Life
is not about ease and met expectations.
A Good Life is a life of fullness.
And fullness comes with pain.

Teach me
to receive
the gift
of disillusionment.

I know it's a hard argument to ignore
because it points to a deeper wound.

But, in this moment,
it's okay to just see
that something hurts in you
and not try to fix it.

You're under the weight
and spell of the Low.

Beloved,
now is not the fullness of Reality.
This season will pass
and there will be
a new day.

Let that new day
be the time
to deal with deep wounds.

Not this moment
in which you're just trying
not to drown in sorrow.

I feel like
I'm attending
a funeral
in my brain.

What has died
is the story
I've been telling myself
about who I am,
what I'm capable of doing
and how my life
is going to turn out.

May the invitation
to "say some words
about the deceased"
be an unexpected
articulation
and revelation
of the story
that is no longer working.

HERE LIES
WHO I AM
WHAT I'M CAPABLE OF DOING
HOW MY LIFE IS GOING TO TURN OUT

I told the story of my Low.
They asked me
"How did you get out?"
I had to tell them the truth.

They came for that,
or at least I assume they did.
They are looking for
the truth about sadness.

They are tired of answers.
So am I. Maybe you are too.
They came to be human.
Maybe you did too.

When the Divine
told the deepest truth,
in the clearest way,
that Truth was human.

So, I told them something
I had only told a few.
"I never got out.
The Low is part of who I am."

I told them that
I carried the sadness
(the one I'd felt trapped in)
up and out and onward.

I told them the truth;
I told them I did not learn
how to get out
of the Low,

I learned
there is Strength in me
for both the valley
and the hilltop.

I think my soul
is tired of
staying invisible
to the rest of humanity.

And if I'm honest
I think
the rest of me
is tired, too.

May this Low inspire me
to get out from under
the exhausting
cloak of invisibility.

May grief and anger
clear the path behind me
so that I may see my past
without the haze of false hope.

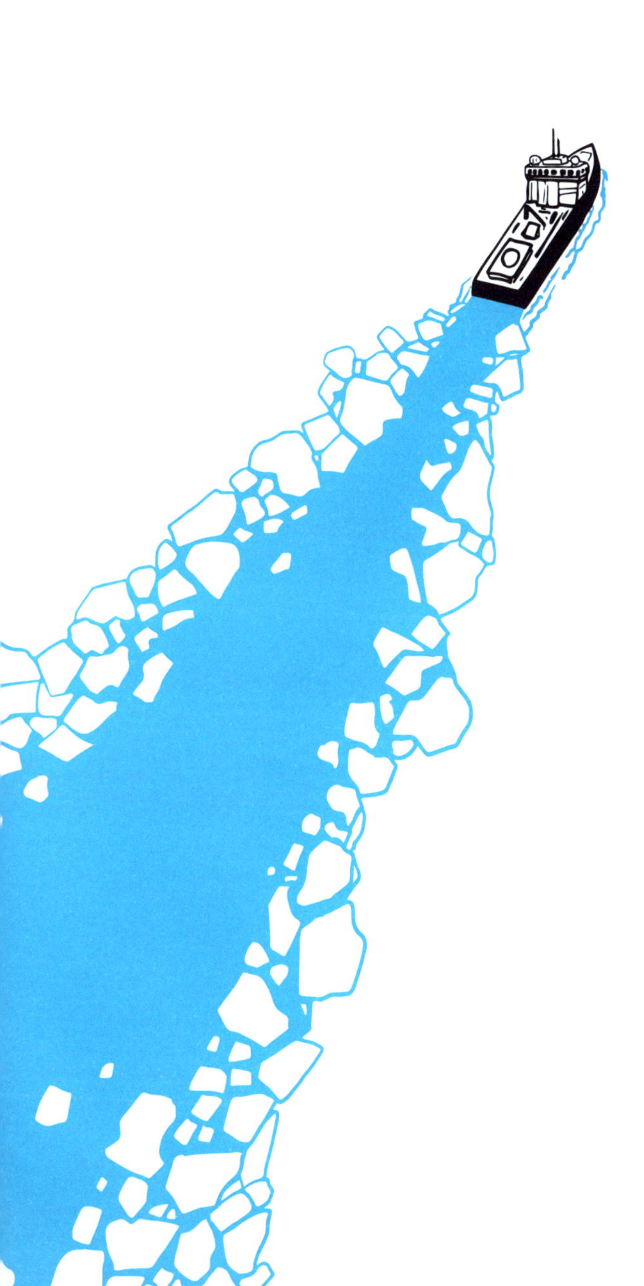

If your house burns down,
how should you feel?

When your favorite pet dies,
how should you feel?

When your favorite sweater finally unravels,
how should you feel?

When you lose
your way
your self
your dream
your hope,
how should you feel?

May the way I feel today
be a way to honor what I've lost
and how much I miss it.

May this Low
help me notice
the marooned
part of me
that has been trying
to get my attention
for a rescue mission.

HELP

We often say,
"It's just my brain"
when actually
we should say,
"Oh no! It's my life!"

Being in the Low
is less about where my head is at
and more about identifying
what my head is in.

Something happened to me.

Help me see
what my head is in.

Be with me
in the untangling.

Comfort me
as I heal.

May the truth

set me free.

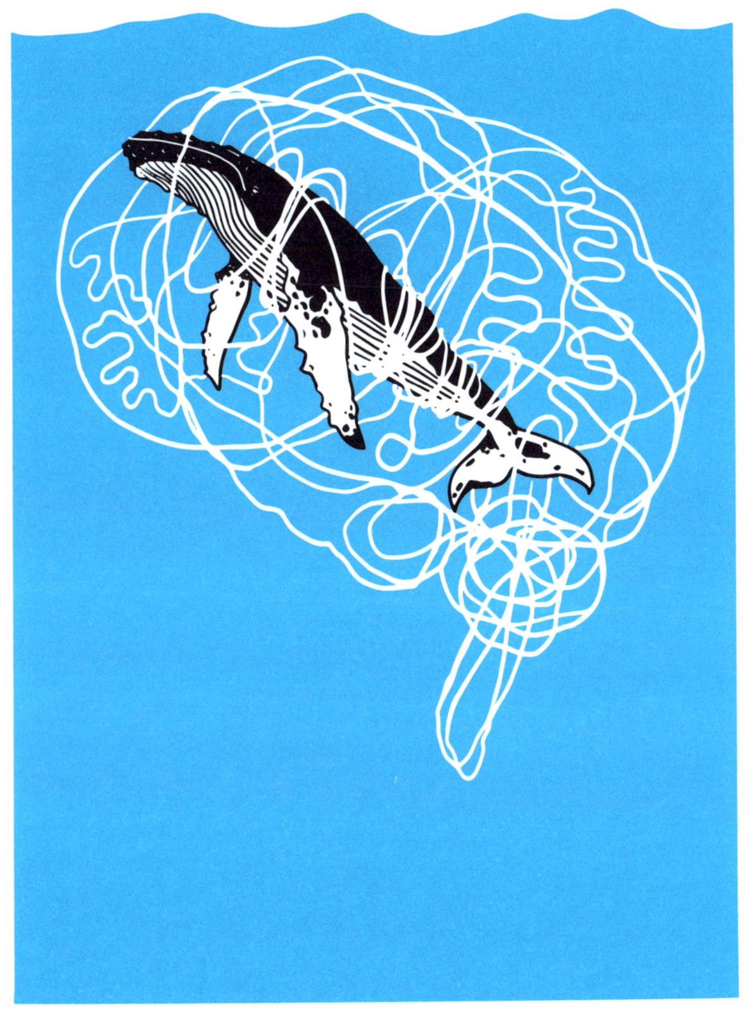

Being known
can feel like being judged.
Being seen
can feel like being condemned.

Remind me that
being loved means vulnerable
and that being vulnerable
means being wound-able.

Protect me from being hurt
by those who might mistreat me
and keep me from the fear of hurt
that keeps me from being open to love.

May I move
from asking
for more wind in my sails
to asking
why I can't cut the anchor.

May being in the Low
equip me
to see
the snag
preventing me
from moving on.

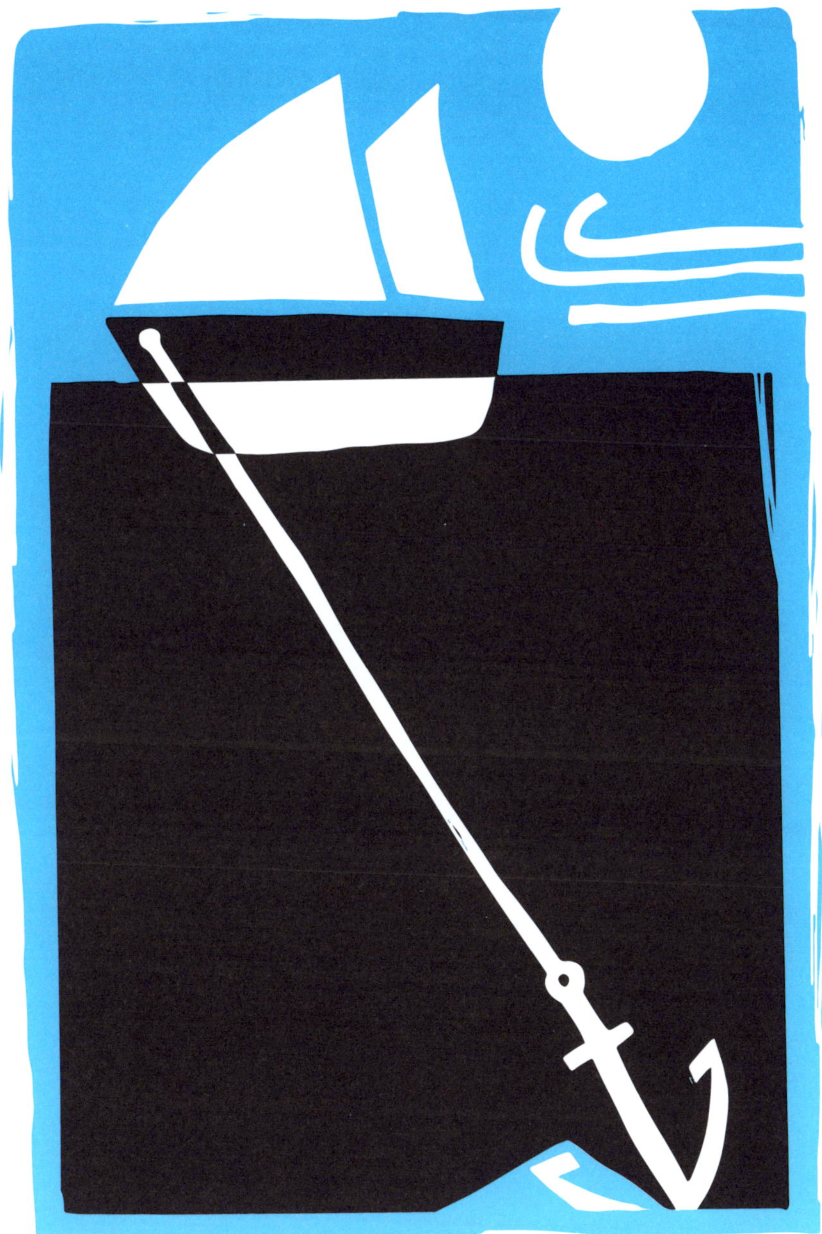

Sadness is a portal and an invitation.
When I am Low
and if I am aware
I can find doorways in the sadness.

Teach me to be here with intention.
Grant me courage
to open my eyes
and examine the landscape of my Low.

Hold me still enough
that my eyes can adjust.
Show me the doorways and windows
in the darkest parts of me.

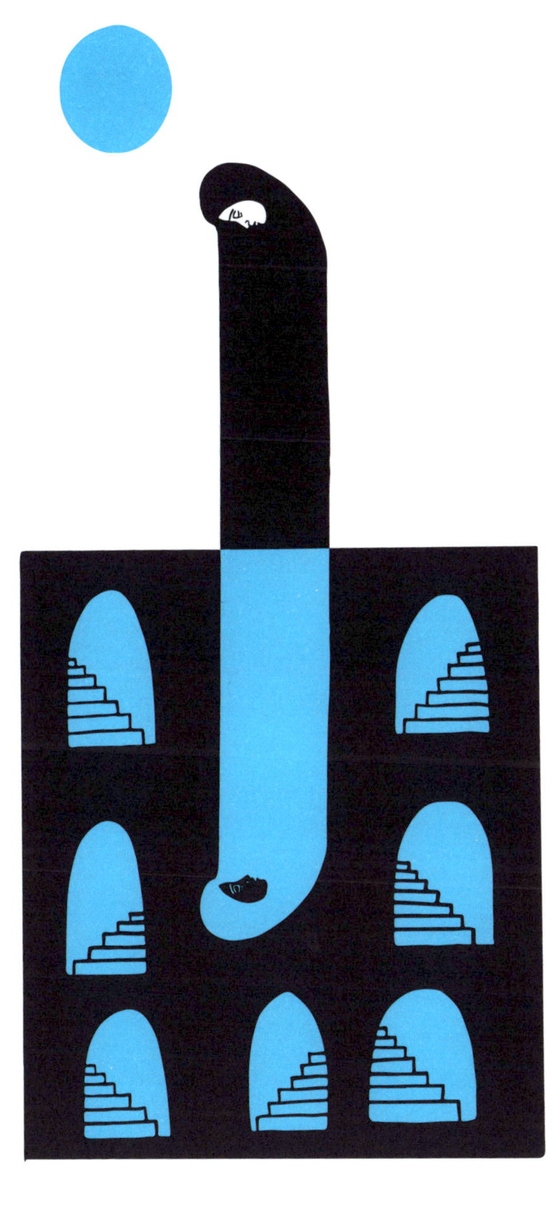

I know when I'm given lemons,
I'm supposed to make lemonade.

And I know I'm supposed to take my pain
and turn it into something useful.

But today,
with the ingredients of my life in front of me,
all I feel like I can make
is a turd sandwich.

Thank you for hearing my honest prayer.

Sometimes I am stuck
because I don't want
what I think is on the other side
of a moment.

Sometimes I am stuck
because I don't want
what I think is on the other side
of the doorway in front of me.

Perhaps more fairly said,
Sometimes I feel stuck
because I think I know the future;
I think I know what comes next.

I don't.

Fear, like a clingy, petulant child,
grasps at my clothing,
holding me hard,
away from the door,

away from my next step
and away from hope.
Grant me the strength
to turn and look

into the face of my childish fear.
Grant me the strength
to lovingly say to myself,
"We are going to be okay."

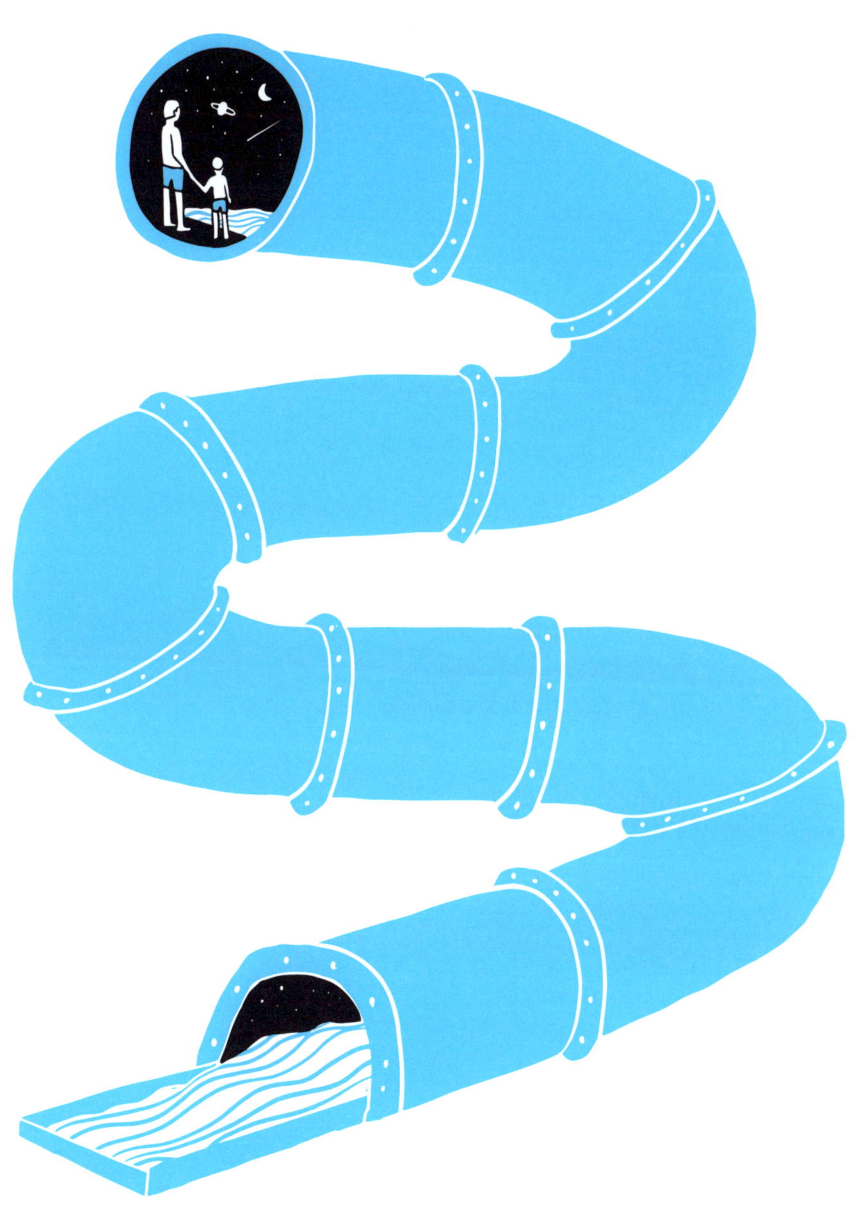

May the terror I feel
at the absence
of what used to be
become hope for what's next.

May my sense of loss
forge a sensitivity in me
to the presence of newness
(or, at least, the hope for it).

Teach me to see
absence as possibility.

If you saw a child
being treated the way
you were treated as a child,
you would do the right thing
and protect that child.

Today, you are being
given the chance
to speak up for that
younger you,
the one who
needed protection
back then.

Depression is like
being trapped in a tornado,
revisiting the same
horrible feeling
over and over again.

May my unfortunate familiarity
with this horrible feeling
evolve with each visitation,
eventually becoming a hospitality
toward the part of me
that wants to heal.

It is confounding
that the Christian notion
of resurrection
carries yesterday with it.

The resurrected body of Jesus
was marked by the scars
of his betrayal,
injury and death.

Resurrection means
carrying my past
without shame
or embarrassment.

Resurrection means that
newness reframes
and redefines
what was.

Resurrection means
I carry my yesterday with me.

I carry my yesterday with me.
Some of that means
holding on to joys
and lessons I cherish.

I carry my yesterday with me.
Some of that means
bearing the marks
of injury, trial, and loss.

I carry my yesterday with me.
Teach me to do so
in a way that
includes all of me.

I've heard it called
"wresting the angel"
or "wrestling with God"
and I suppose that's what I'm doing.

I've needed things
I didn't feel You were providing.
I've wanted things
I didn't feel You were giving.

So I did what I could
to take hold of You, saying
"I will not let You go
unless You bless me."

But again
You did not give me
what I came for.
Instead, You renamed me.

And now
everything is different,
including what I want
and what I need.

And maybe
that's what I've been chasing
all this time:
Newness.

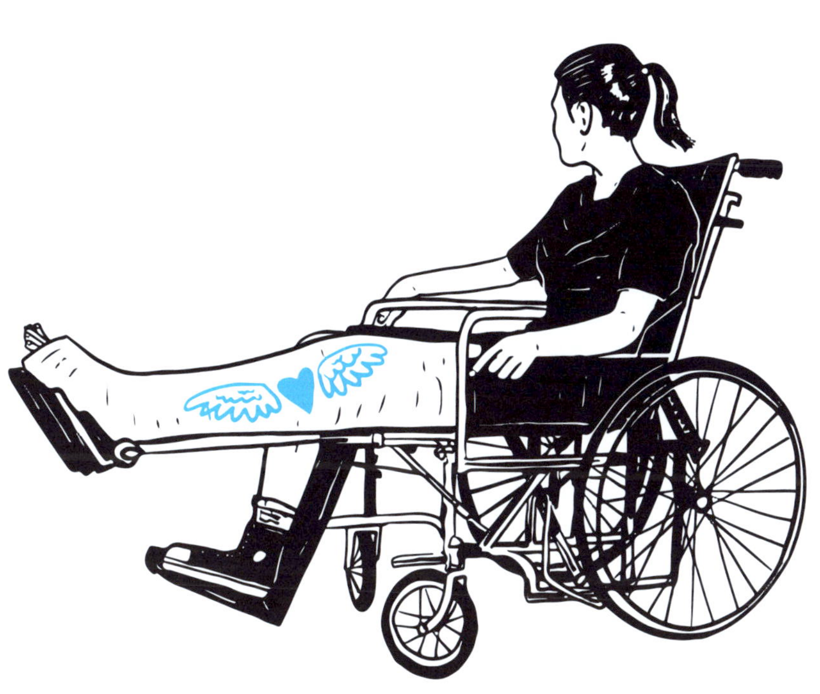

# Reconnecting to
# What I Am a Part Of

## Considering the Disconnection from the Natural World and Status and Respect

South of where I live by just over an hour is Henry Cowell State Park. The park features redwood trees that are upward of 1,600 years old. For some perspective, only seven nations on earth are older than these trees. Toward the back of the park is a redwood you can climb into and stand fully upright. The tree's roots have grown to provide a doorway, complete with a small staircase leading down into the earth. During a recent visit, as I was waiting my turn to enter the tree, I watched a younger man wearing a very nice business suit smack his head on the tree while climbing out. The crowd gathered around the tree gave a collective "Ouch" while the young man staggered a bit. The park docent reached out to steady him, adding, "You hit your head pretty hard, son."

"I'm so sorry! Did I hurt the tree?"

The docent smiled. "Oh, the tree doesn't even know you're here. Are *you* okay?"

That's quite a thing to hear, isn't it? That you weren't noticed. Especially as a message of comfort. Yet I wonder if that's part of what draws us to the slow rhythms and indifference of nature: the desire to feel small. I wonder if, instead of always feeling powerful and needed, our souls want to regularly feel small, insignificant, and desired.

I know many of us have felt minimized or cast out at times. But what if there's a gift available, even in that? What if one of the deep lessons of life is that the stories we are trying to fit into aren't sufficient? What if being rejected by lesser stories opens us up to an invitation to find a story large enough, good enough, and beautiful enough to hold all of us? What if the story we actually belong to is too big for us to know all of it, and we aren't its main character? What if the story our souls long for is one in which we are quite small?

Of course, there are different kinds of smallness. One is the smallness offered by utility, in which I must minimize myself in order to be a productive, useful part of a story that needs my energies for its ends. The other kind of smallness comes from knowing that, as expansive as my life might ever be, the Story I am part of is bigger, older, wilder, and more beautiful than my most sweeping imaginings, a Story in which I can stand up as tall as I want and stretch out with every bit of chaotic, inspired energy in me and *still* be a welcomed part of a sacred reality. I wonder if part of why we often feel so cramped and tense is that the narratives we try to fit ourselves into just aren't enough for our divinely crafted human souls.

Being "Mom" or "Dad" or "Patriot."

Being "Friend" or "Artist" or "Radical."

Any of these stories might be good stories. But I wonder if they're still too small. In an interview for Absolute Motivation, actor and comedian Jim Carrey said it this way:

> Depression is your body saying . . . "I don't want to be this character anymore, I don't want to hold up this avatar that you've created in the world. It's too much for me."[4]

We don't have what it takes to be the main character in our own lives. We're not designed with that capacity. A story in which we are the main character doesn't have room for the One to Whom Every Story Belongs—the One to Whom We Belong.

I do need to know I'm part of Something Bigger. But the Bigger Story I am designed to live in is one I am too small to comprehend, much less control. I can smell a hint of it in the scent of night jasmine, and I can catch a whisper of it if I breathe among the sequoias. I can feel my pulse slow to its rhythms if I stand waist-deep in the ocean. And I notice that I am not *necessary* in any of these places. Which makes me wonder if part of why I feel so disjointed is because I've been trying to be so integral.

> I wasn't created
> to be necessary.
> I wasn't created
> out of necessity.
>
> I was created out of desire
> so that I might know
> I am desired
> and welcomed.

I felt this when I crossed the finish line after the 26.2 miles of my first (and maybe only) marathon. I was exhausted, exhilarated, and abundantly proud of myself. The feeling of personal accomplishment was a rich reward for the grind of the race itself, as well as for the work I'd put in over the many previous months. I let my jog become a slow walk, turning my face to the sky like a satellite dish receiving blissful signals of joy. That bliss was gently interrupted by the gleeful voice of a race volunteer: "Congratulations, Runner! You did it!" As she reached toward me with a finisher's medal, I thought to myself,

I'm a Runner.
I'm *actually* a Runner.
"They" said so.
I just got a medal from
The International Society of People Who Run.
I'm one of "Them."
That means
I'm a Runner!

This elation was different from what I'd felt crossing the finish line alone. It was the thrill of being seen and acknowledged, of being welcomed. I was being met in my need and desire to be a part of Something Bigger. Sure, I'd run the 26.2 to celebrate my own body and "prove" I could do it.

## But/And

I'd run at a particular time in a particular place so that I could share the experience with other people—and be acknowledged, be received. I wanted to be seen.

I have come to despise the way hyperindividualist narratives from film and television have characterized the desire to be respected or have status among peers as a form of weakness or even a character fault. That's such garbage! The truth is this:

There are essential aspects
of my identity
that can only be given to me
by other people.

In the same way my soul is designed to find context in the cosmic history of the world God created, my soul is also designed to be nourished by the loving attention and admiration of others. A disconnection from the status and respect others offer can leave us feeling more than just alone. Without them, we wither; we feel incomplete spiritually, socially, and emotionally.

It seems, at least at times, we don't take this disconnection seriously enough. We play a game with it instead, one a lot like Marco Polo.

- We are propelled by the desire and need to find someone else in the pool.
- We are unable to see.
- We are almost entirely dependent upon other people to help us find them.
- We feel silly and incapable while other people are toying with our efforts to connect.

In the actual pool of life-with-others, I'm never just the kid with their eyes closed, working to connect and belong. I'm also one of the kids with their eyes open, hearing the calls of the disconnected. I think that's where the tide can turn, if we're willing. That's where my prayers have been directed, at least. I want to be someone who is easier to find in the pool. I think that's how the cycle of contempt and isolation gets broken; when, even if I've been disrespected and dismissed, I work to offer you respect and status simply because I know you need them like I do.

After I'd finished that marathon, I was one of those goofy runner nerds who wore their race medal well into the night. I changed out of my running shorts and shirt because I smelled like I'd been dragged across the floor of a junior high school gym. But the medal stayed. For hours and through two outfit changes, I nodded and smiled at other runners who *also* wore their medals while we got coffee and tequila and ice cream (the rewards of distance running). Some of those folks finished hours before me. Some finished after I did. But our belonging was entirely predicated on our shared struggle. The medal from The International Society of People Who Run served as an invitation of sorts. It said,

"We did this together. I see you. I receive you."

> You weren't created
> to be necessary.
> You weren't created
> out of necessity.
>
> You were created out of desire
> so that you might know
> you are desired
> and sought after.

Let's pray.

*Welcome, welcome, welcome.*
*I welcome everything that comes to me today, because I know it's for my healing.*
*I welcome all thoughts, feelings, emotions, persons, situations, and conditions.*
*I let go of my desire for power and control.*
*I let go of my desire for affection, esteem, approval, and pleasure.*
*I let go of my desire for survival and security.*
*I let go of my desire to change any situation, condition, person or myself.*
*I open to the love and presence of God and God's action within.*
*Amen.*

I am told
my body will last only seventy-four years
on an earth that has seen
fifty-three million of my lifetimes.

Teach me the peace
of knowing
I am not everything.
Nor am I nothing.

Remind me that,
far better than being needed,
I am precious
and cherished.

Rescue me from the trap
of being important.
Relieve me of the weight
that comes with being necessary.

May you remember
that everyone
at some point
needs to be carried.

Not everyone
thinks you're
a waste of space
the way you do
when you're in the depths
of the Low.

It's just your turn
to allow someone else
to care for a friend.

It's not absurd
for members of the first species
who are aware of the scope of terrors in the universe
to have an "off day."

The miracle of existence
is a sacred humiliation,
a holy terror,
a paradoxical blessing,
a benevolent fluke
and an impossible mystery.

I am a part of this
impossible mystery.

May this "off day"
be an unexpected invitation
to feel, in my body,
the miracle of
my mysterious existence.

Help me slow the pace
of my walking and breathing and thinking
and attune my body
to the ever-present rhythms around me.

Teach me these rhythms
that were set in motion
by the hand of God
at the beginning of all things.

May I have the same wonder
in the gift of my existence
as I do when I look at the stars
because I am,
in fact,
made of
the same
glorious elements.

It takes so long
for my heartbeat to slow
so I can feel air reach
the bottom of my lungs.

I am practiced at
taking in only enough breath
to push the next thought
from my mouth.

Teach me to breathe
like the trees.
Teach me the long,
slow repetition of

I am,
I am,
I am,
I am.

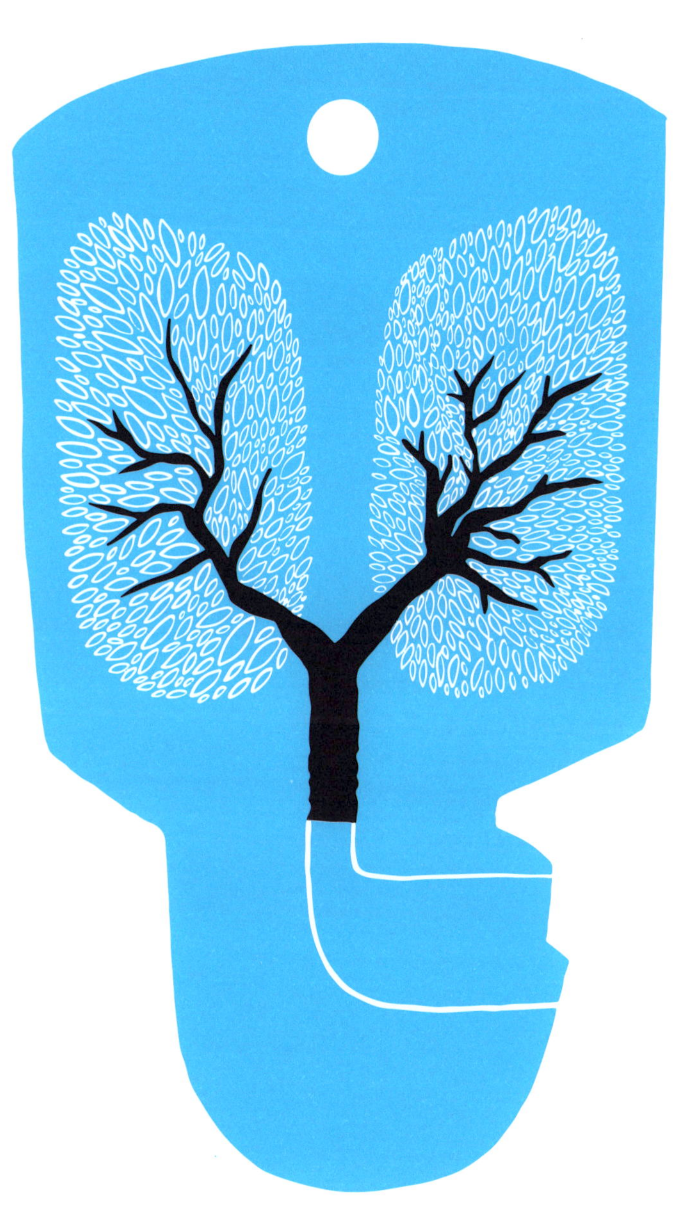

If I were to sit at a beach
for a long time
I'd see that the ocean
looks a lot like my life.

Moments of excitement
amid the long steady
rotation of the tides.

I'm reminded of the ever-changing
ebb and flow of life.

Just as tides are high
and then low,
I trust that this Low
will not last forever.

May I be reminded
that life is seasonal
and I am not alone.

The very trees see my Fall
and offer their solidarity
in the vulnerable process
of transforming.

I am trained and tempted
to think and feel
that I exist
at the center of my life.

But in the Low

I am learning

the weight of being the center

is too much.

May the indifference of the wind
softly displace me from the middle
of the story I'm telling myself
about the life I'm given.

May the impossible
depth and breadth of the ocean
minimize the space
I think I take up.

Help me embrace my smallness
so that, in my limitation,
I can feel seen
and wanted and loved.

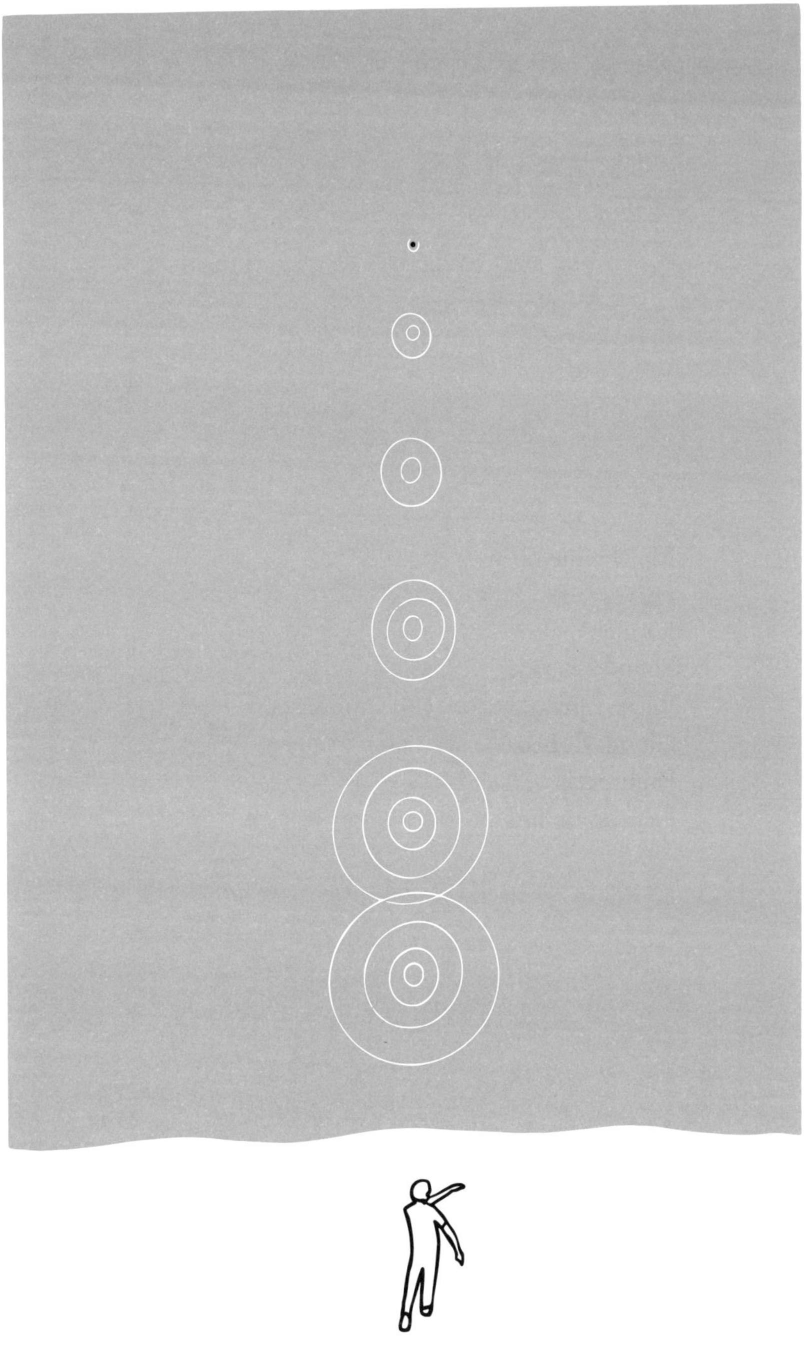

May I remember . . .
Leaves fall.
Ice melts.
Footprints fade.
Waves retreat.
Clouds disperse.
Paint peels.
Depression lifts.

I have heard it said
that faith is not
a cognitive acquiescence
to the idea that You are Good.

Faith is
taking steps
when I am unsure
of Your Goodness.

Get me out of my head,
back in my body
and in touch with my heart
with my mind in the mix.

Remind me that faith
is movement
and that movement
is an embodied act of conscious will.

May I remember
that being kind
to others
is the greatest
antidepressant.

Have mercy
on the ones who love me
when I am Low
for they know not what to do.

Be kind
to the ones who care for me
when I am not well.
I can be so cruel.

I don't always ask
for what I truly need
and I sometimes reject
good help.

Have mercy on those
who work to find me
when I am lost
and do not want to be found.

I know I need them.
I know I am not
fully myself
without them.

So, have mercy on me.
I forget and mistreat
the ones who love me
even as I forget and mistreat myself.

In moments of fear and uncertainty,
grant me the courage to face life's terrors
with an open heart.

Help me embrace these challenges,
believing it is through experiencing the depths of fear
that I can truly appreciate and marvel
at the wonders life has to offer.

May I find strength, resilience, and awe
in the contrast of life's terrors and wonders,
knowing that they are interwoven
in the tapestry of my existence.

Some things
can't be healed
without
the help of others.

Today
may I remember
that I can't heal
by myself.

That is
an unexpected gift
awaiting me
as I get in touch with
my deeper wounds.

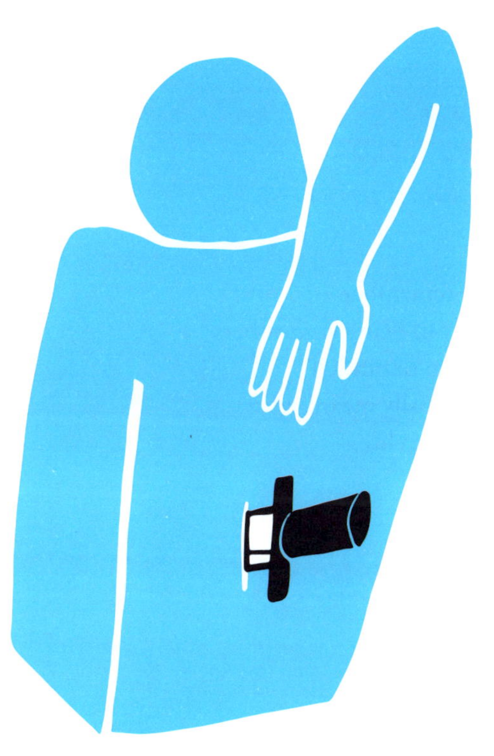

May I remember
it's only in being with others
that I am reminded
what is really meaningful
to a human life.

Most people
don’t put “deep friendships”
on their bucket list.

But most people,
before they kick the bucket,
say one of their greatest regrets
was losing touch
with their friends.

May this Low
remind me of
the Grand Tour
available to me
in an everyday life
adventured with
close friends.

END
OF THE
ROAD

This melancholic chapter
is not my whole story
but a valuable section
in the book of my life;
one that surprisingly becomes
the part most relatable
to the whole world.

Rescue me
from the weight of being essential.
Remind me instead
that I am wanted and chosen.

Grant me courage
to open my eyes in the dark
and see the landscape
of the Low.

Teach me to know sadness
as an invitation
to something else,
something my soul longs for.

Hold me still enough
to let my eyes adjust,
that I might see

paths and doorways and windows.

Teach me
to be here
with intention
and peace.

Teach me to listen.
Tune my soul like an instrument.
I want to resonate
with Your Song.

When I offer myself
to the world
You've given me to,
I long to hear You say,

"You are mine.
I love you.
I'm proud
of you."

No human life is perfect
and each has its own
unique shape.

May this Low
allow me to appreciate
my life

and its unique,
one of a kind
shape.

My hope is not
that the dark corners of my soul
are vanquished
by floods of light.

My hope is that
when I am in
those darker corners,
I still feel at home.

May I lovingly recognize
the aspects of me
that live and grow
here in the Low.

Because the valley is in me,
that must mean
there is more to me
than I can see when I'm in it.

Grant me
the courage to believe
this valley is a small part
of my large life.

# Reconnecting to **What I Value**

## Considering the Disconnection from Meaningful Work and Intrinsic Values

The most nauseated I've ever been was on (and after) a carnival ride called the Gravitron. If you've never braved a traveling carnival, the Gravitron is basically a salad spinner for people. Instead of extracting water droplets from lettuce leaves, the Gravitron extracts equilibrium from human bodies. In the interest of full disclosure, you should know that, on the night in question, I'd eaten a hot dog, a funnel cake, and a large popcorn before boarding the ride, washing it all down with a root beer roughly the size of my head. It was entirely reasonable for my body to feel terrible. I'm not designed to eat that much junk and then be twirled around at various angles for a minute and a half.

At times, my relationship with the world around me and its values can feel a bit like being on the Gravitron—sideways and nauseatingly chaotic. This statistical collision is a decent example: At the time of this writing, over 35 percent of the human population lives in moderate to severe poverty.[5] Without getting into the statistical weeds, we're talking about billions of people, most of them children, trying their best to survive on less than $3.00 a day. That's not how I think the world should work. I don't think kids should go without food because they were born in the "wrong" zip code. Meanwhile, my country's government spent nearly $17 billion in 2023 updating our nuclear arsenal[6] (devices we've created with the hope of not using them), and my country's citizens spent over $850 billion on Christmas gifts, as we do every year.[7]

The collision of these statistical realities creates a significant tension in me that sounds like this: If we were to take a single percentage point from each of those spending totals (I'm literally talking about 1 or 2 percent), we could go a very long way toward feeding every hungry mouth on the planet and breaking the poverty cycle for roughly one billion children.

I've been told I'm naive and unreasonable for thinking this way. I'm told that matters of poverty, consumer spending, and foreign policy simply "are what they are," and my childlike sensibilities don't have a place in the Adult World. I've often felt like the values I most deeply identify with mean I don't identify very deeply with the world I'm living in. The trouble is, I can't help but feel the way I do about the things I sincerely value, and that leaves me somewhat stuck. I used to wish I could contort my soul to adopt the postures of my environment and stop feeling sad and crazy so often.

> I just can't do that.
> I guess I've read
> too many comics.

In *The Amazing Spider-Man* #537, Captain America, during a moment of cultural and political upheaval, says to a conflicted Peter Parker,

> Doesn't matter what the press says. Doesn't matter what the politicians or the mobs say. Doesn't matter if the whole country decides something wrong is something right. This nation was founded on one principle above all else: the requirement that we stand up for what we believe, no matter the odds or

> the consequences. When the mob and the press and the whole world tell you to move, your job is to plant yourself like a tree beside the river of truth, and tell the world, "No. You move."[8]

The prevalence of anxiety and depression is more than just a personal problem shared by millions of people with soft hearts. It is also an indictment of the systems and dominant ideologies around us. In other words, it's not just a matter of what's in our heads; it's also a matter of what our heads are in. Yes, we've got work to do, internally. But that's not all of why we feel disoriented.

During the vault portion of the women's gymnastics competition at the 2000 Summer Olympics, several athletes in a row landed oddly. Many couldn't land their vaults at all. Initially, broadcasters wondered if these young women were compromised by their own nerves, as this was the first Olympic experience for many of them. But after seeing two rotations of athletes struggle, Australian gymnast Allana Slater suggested something was wrong with the vault itself. She was right. The vault horse had been set to 120 cm instead of the Olympic standard of 125 cm.[9] The problem wasn't the gymnasts or their skills, it was the equipment. In fact, the stumbling and struggling of the participants was evidence that something about the system was crooked.

I think it's more than fair to say the prevalence of depression and anxiety is evidence that much of the world around us is crooked; we've been set up poorly. The percentage of adults who currently report living with depression is almost 10 percentage points higher than a decade ago, sitting just below 30 percent.[10] And while we can point at an array of societal factors contributing to that trend (the turbulence of social media networks, twenty-four-hour cycles of fear narratives posing as "news," etc.), one thing is clear: We are having a very similar experience to that of those gymnasts in 2000, an experience of a world that is dangerously discordant with human flourishing.

Of course, there's a significant difference between that Olympic moment and the one you and I are in. Olympic gymnasts trust their bodies and minds to tell them the truth about their environment because they've trained well and responsibly for years. Because they're in excellent condition, a great gymnast knows when the vault horse is off-kilter, even by as little as 5 cm. They also know when their own bodies are "off" or when their wrists aren't locked completely during a vault or when they've not stretched well enough. That kind of awareness just isn't as true for you and me most of the time.

While I'm not suggesting we must spiritually and emotionally train with the intensity of Olympic gymnasts, I am definitely saying that, given the crookedness of our environment, we must take our own well-being far more seriously. We might be getting spun around, Gravitron-style, by agencies and agendas whose values are antithetical to our health, but it's also likely we fed ourselves spiritual and emotional junk food before getting on their ride. I am not just a person at odds with the world's system of values; I am also at odds with my own values.

I'm the one who bought the phone I spend too much time on.
I'm the one who downloaded the apps that feed me insecurity and competition.
I'm the one who cut that relationship off instead of doing the work of forgiveness and reconciliation.
I'm the one who took the safe job when it was time to take a risk.
I'm the one who hits snooze more than once in the morning.

I want to be more like those Olympic athletes who are so in tune with their bodies they notice when things are even slightly off and can name the problem, making way for a fix. I want to be like a tree planted by the river of truth, helping calm the turbulence of a world seemingly committed to undoing itself. That means I have to reckon with (I know you saw this coming) the Gravitron in me. Yes, I want to work to redeem and transform the systems and ideologies I believe are leveled against us. I also need to confess that I willingly join forces with them far too often; that I am at odds with my very own soul at times and "*I do not understand what I do. For what I want to do I do not do, but what I hate I do.*"[11]

I want a more stable and peaceful world.
I want a more stable and peaceful me.
For both of those, I need help.
Thank God help is available.

Help me to seek
and receive that help
in the places
it is being offered.

In communities of people,
some of whom are unlike me,
who are committed to not give up meeting together
as some are in the habit of doing.

In trained professionals
who can help me find
the five-centimeter flaw
in the way I've set my life up.

In great works of literature
(including *The Amazing Spider-Man* #537)
that help us locate ourselves
when everything seems to be spinning out of control.

And always in the One
whose Way was so counter
to the world's systems and values
that the mobs and the politicians

and the whole world conspired
to label him problematic
and wrong-headed,
and then have him killed.

Let's pray.

*Welcome, welcome, welcome.*
*I welcome everything that comes to me today, because I know it's for my healing.*
*I welcome all thoughts, feelings, emotions, persons, situations, and conditions.*
*I let go of my desire for power and control.*
*I let go of my desire for affection, esteem, approval, and pleasure.*
*I let go of my desire for survival and security.*
*I let go of my desire to change any situation, condition, person or myself.*
*I open to the love and presence of God and God's action within.*
*Amen.*

May I know that,
some days,
I cannot tune in
to the meaning of life.

That does not mean
I cannot know other
good and deep things
about being alive.

What if
it's all really complex
and you're not crazy
or broken or stupid?

What if your sadness
can be trusted
to share in how hard
it can be to be alive?

What if part of
what makes you sane,
whole and intelligent
is your grief?

May it be so
that we can trust
our time in the Low
to tell us where we are

especially when
where we are
is not
altogether good.

My grief is not an illness.
My grief honors me
by reminding me
that I have loved.

My grief is not a problem.
My grief honors those I have loved
when they are gone.
They are worth hurting for.

Teach me to let my grief
be a friend to my memory,
that I might taste the sweetness
sadness adds to the past.

May I remember
I'm not the only
one who has
found himself in the Low.

Humans have left all kinds
of artifacts from their Low
as a way to help others
when they find themselves here.

Art, books, movies, poetry
are all helpful
crutches to lean on
when one feels they cannot muster
the strength to do so.

Today,
I am grateful
for others who took the time
to make something out of their pain.

There may even be a day
when I add
a helpful artifact
to this library of solidarity.

mystery
FICTION
physics
ASTRONOMY
STORY
ART
memoir
comedy
poetry
TRAVEL
FILM
PAINTING
JOURNAL
love songs
GARDENING
WOOD WORKING
POTTERY
MUSIC
origami
sculpture
welding

I do not understand
the emotional alchemy
that turns care
into worry.

Perhaps it has to do
with the sheer weight of things;
there is so much (too much)
to care about.

Perhaps care
is crushed and compressed,
becoming something much smaller
and less spacious.

Perhaps this is
the dark weight
under which
dread is born.

May I spend less time
worrying about
"the things I have to deal with"
or "the things I need to do."

May I give more time to
actually dealing with
and doing
those things.

May aspiration
never blind me
to the actual fruits
of my work.

May I never numb
to the sacred gift it is
to work
at all.

Awaken me
to the enjoyment of
my own strength
and my own ability.

Stir in me an awareness
of my fortune;
I am a participant
in the renewal of all things.

Because I do not stop
until I am worn out or injured,
the only time
I take a long look at my life
is when I'm in the dark.

Seeing this way
distorts my vision
for the gift it is
to be alive.

Teach me
to pause
when all is light,
simple and easy.

Teach me to reflect
the way I do
when I am down here
in the Low.

Sometimes,
we are given glimpses
into the enormity of the work at hand.
Not so that we might increase our capacity
to do a larger work or more work

but so that the work
we are already doing
would become more vital
and less optional.

Rescue me
from overwhelm.
I cannot do
all I want to do.

May I be

compelled and moved
to do the work
I can do.

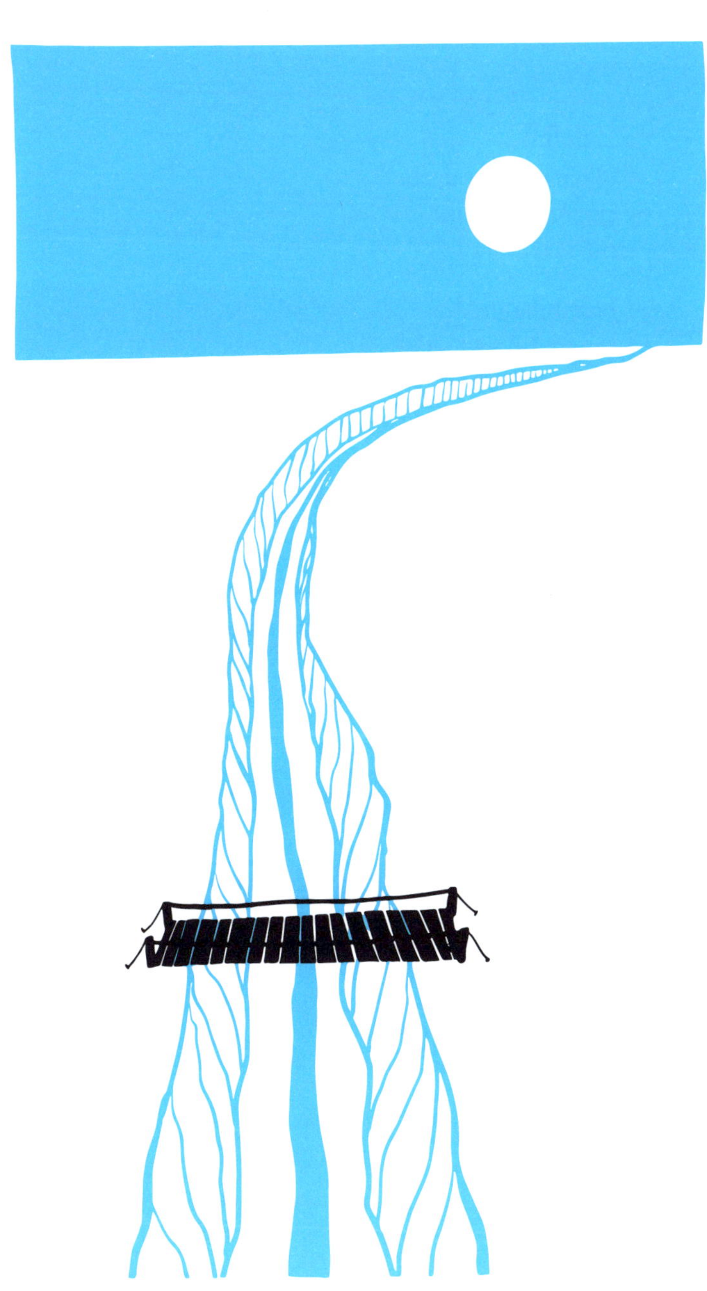

I am full
of clicks and buzzes
emanating from
the machines I use.

I am inhabited
(or am I possessed?)
by these tools
and my need for them.

Like a metronome
keeping a time
out of step
with my pulse,

out of sync
with my circadian rhythms
and at odds
with my hunger.

I am full
of clicks and buzzes.
I am out of rhythm
with myself.

Teach me to attend,
patiently and deeply enough,
to hear the soft beat
of my human heart.

May I see the way
all the various
colors in me
provide the elements
of a complex composition,

even though
some are colors
I tend not
to favor.

It's in the contrast
that the composition
comes to life.

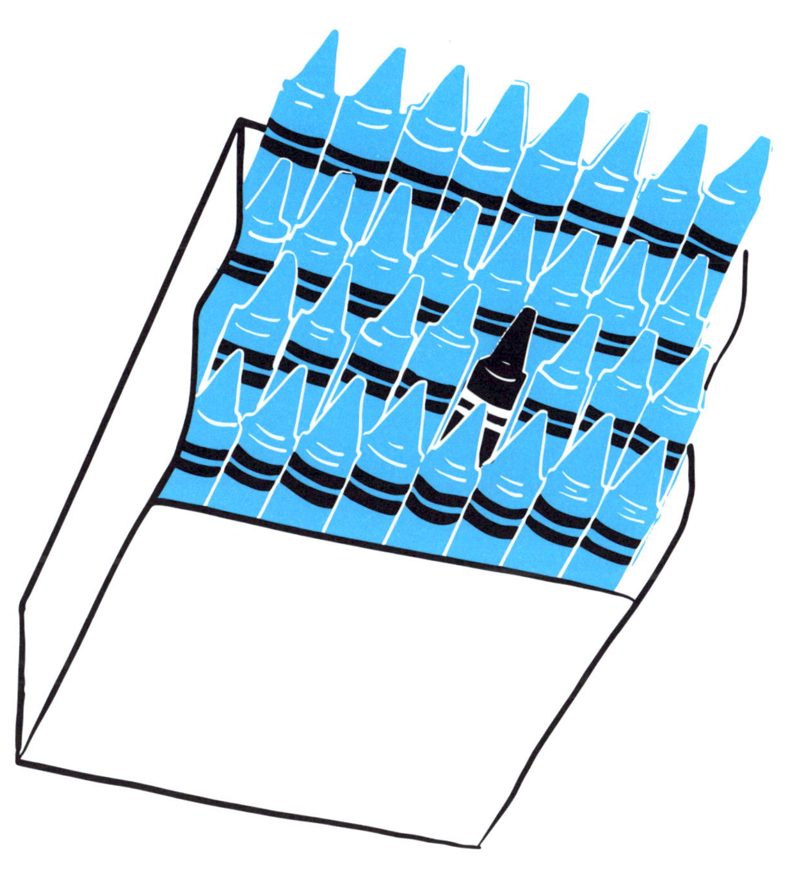

May I be reminded
that the opposite of death scrolling
is life noticing

and that this Low
has made me notice
parts of my life
I've scrolled past
for too long.

May I have wisdom and patience
to follow the signs
my disappointments
leave for me.

I want to learn
to trust my saddened soul
to tell me truths
I might not learn otherwise.

Teach me to feel disappointment
as the way my soul tells me
"I want(ed) something else;
I want(ed) something better."

Remind me I'm still learning.
Remind me I'm still becoming.
Remind me I'm not done yet
and I can choose more wisely tomorrow.

Sometimes, I hunger
because I do not eat what is offered.
Some of why I lack
is because I resist the gift being given.

I lift my eyes up
only to the hills I choose;
I want to choose
where my help comes from.

May my particularities
and my preferences
never cut me off
from the Life available to me.

Forgive me for choosing "my way."
It seemed right
but I fear it is
leading me toward death.

Teach me to feed on
what You prepare for me.
Teach me to receive
what You generously give.

May the very depth and intensity
of my own grief
sever the ties that bind me
to my preferences and privilege.

May my time in the Low
clear the debris
of attachment and ego
so that I can be cared for.

My longings
are part of who I am.
They propel me outward
and energize me to create.

My imaginings
are part of who I am.
They draw me inward
to see the beauty of my own soul.

These longings and imaginings
do not align
with the ways and agendas
of a mechanized world.

I experience that misalignment
as stress and disconnection.

Teach me
to receive my own
lust for life
as a gift.

Regardless of
the resistance I experience
from systems and entities
that do not want me well.

The richest gift
available to me in work
is not what I achieve
but who I become.

Grant me the eyes
to see myself in my labors
and to sense the active way
You're forming me in them.

Grant me some small sense
of Your pleasure in me
even as I work at things
I struggle to take pleasure in.

Weakness is evidence
that I have spent my strength.
Sadness is evidence
that I love my life.

Teach me to see
being depleted
as a sign
of being alive.

Sadness is a portal and an invitation.
When I am Low (and if I am aware)
I can find doorways
in the sadness.

Teach me to be here with intention.
Grant me courage
to open my eyes
and examine the landscape of my Low.

Hold me still enough
to let my eyes adjust.
Show me the doorways and windows
in the darkest parts of me.

May I grow
to know my sadness
as an absence,

one that points
toward the Presence
my soul longs for.

Teach me to not fear
the feeling of emptiness
that invariably sets in
when I set down lesser hopes.

May I become soft enough
to hope for (and even celebrate)
change and restoration
in systems I've most vehemently criticized.

Teach me to desire goodness
in the lives of those
with whom I have experienced
my deepest disappointments.

Keep me from the lie
that I am what I do
and that I am only whole
when I achieve my goals.

Keep me from the lie
that I am corrupted by my labors
and that I am only whole
in stillness and rest.

When expedience
is the distinguishing mark
of the work I do,
I treat myself like a machine.

Teach me to be
the person
I dreamt of being
when the dream of God
awakened in me.

BE STILL AND KNOW THAT I AM GOD

BE STILL AND KNOW THAT I AM

BE STILL AND KNOW
BE STILL

BE

I spent so much time
working to be a world changer.
I forged myself into
the most useful instrument.

I had hope that
I would be used
by powerful hands
to "make a difference."

But I wear out
and I tire of labor.
My exhaustion renders me
ill-fit for use.

In the Low,
I make no change
and I make
little difference.

In the Low,
I hope and long
to be rescued and helped
by kind and careful hands.

Remind me
that there is more to me
than my usefulness
and my strength.

Teach me
that achievement
is too small a thing
to contain a human soul.

Rescue me
from the smallness of mind
that allows me to be allured
    and captured
by agendas that require me
    to be usable.

May my time
in the Low
help cure me of my addiction
to accomplishment.

Show me that I am
loved in strength and in
    weakness.
That kind of Love
actually changes things.

The fear of doing the task
is almost always worse
than the pain I experience
while doing the task.

May the work of my hands
be a celebration
of the power I have
over almost everything that worries me.

May the practice of work
become the path
of freedom
from dread.

you got this.

Maybe being in tune
with our modern world
means having the blues
is inevitable.

But the surprise
of this inevitability
is growing in the faculty
to alchemize
pain into hope,
turn nothing into something,
make isolation into solidarity
and transform chaos into song.

May I remember
that every great song
is about the wildness
of the human condition

and this Low
is just one way
to be a songwriter
in this global band.

# Reconnecting to What Is Ahead of Me

## Considering the Disconnection from a Hopeful Future

On the first day of second grade, in September 1981, I took a brown paper lunch sack to school that featured a crude drawing of Libya's chair of the revolutionary command council in crosshairs. Underneath, I'd written "Kill Kadaffi."

Muammar al-Qaddafi (not Kadaffi) had been identified by then-president Ronald Reagan as a "Soviet puppet" and was therefore a representative of the most feared and hated entity in the collective American psyche: The Russians. His very existence threatened our way of life, and he needed to be wiped from the face of the earth.

My parents, both born in the 1930s, had grown up in the shadow of nuclear fear. On any given day, Russia might fire off a nuclear attack to which the United States would have to respond, resulting in the annihilation of civilization as we knew it. Before *that*, my grandparents were born on the eve of WWI and then spent their twenties being pelted by WWII newsreels and propaganda.

> For my family,
> there has always
> been a Threat.
>
> Some Entity is "out there"
> planning and plotting to hurt us
> and to steal from us our future.

Before I knew how to think, I'd adopted the narrative that the future was perpetually under threat and that the only hope was some form of violence. So, in lockstep with my cultural tradition, I pulled a liverwurst sandwich out of a paper sack upon which I'd poorly drawn a death threat against a Libyan dictator and profoundly misspelled his name. That's one of the tricks Fear plays: It convinces us to trade hope for an angry, controlling version of Practicality. Fear says, "If you don't kill the thing chasing you, it will kill you."

Hope, on the other hand, sees everything Fear sees, recognizes those same threats and takes them just as seriously, but does so with the sobriety of history and with peace in her heart.

> Hope says,
> "It is likely
> things are
> actually worse
> than we know them to be.
>
> It is also likely
> Goodness is far more enduring,
> and far more available,
> than we have imagined."

Hope does not ignore the darkness and the Low. Hope stands next to me in it, constant and unwavering. Hope holds my wrist while perils and menaces swirl around. Hope waits patiently for me to stop shaking and then pulls me kindly in the direction of my next step—toward light and toward Vision.

Hope gives birth to Vision. Vision isn't about knowing the future; it is about actively creating the future regardless of our circumstances and obstacles. And far better than the ability to predict tomorrow's outcomes, Vision is the willingness and capacity to work toward goodness and beauty with whatever we have on hand. Vision is the thing Fear most vehemently abhors. Because Vision is unbothered by brokenness and incompletion. Vision knows she'll not only make do with the dregs; she'll make wine from it. Vision infuses a human heart with the electricity of potentiality so that those of us who live with Hope can say,

> "I don't care
> what's coming next,
> and I'm not concerned
> with how pretty or ugly it is.
>
> I will take whatever I'm given
> and make from it
> things more beautiful
> than you can imagine."

Let's pray.

*Welcome, welcome, welcome.*
*I welcome everything that comes to me today, because I know it's for my healing.*
*I welcome all thoughts, feelings, emotions, persons, situations, and conditions.*
*I let go of my desire for power and control.*
*I let go of my desire for affection, esteem, approval, and pleasure.*
*I let go of my desire for survival and security.*

*I let go of my desire to change any situation, condition, person or myself.*
*I open to the love and presence of God and God's action within.*
*Amen.*

Remind me
that being is becoming
and that who I am
is not a conclusion.

Teach me that existence
is a conversation
in which I get to ask
questions like "What if . . . ?"

May I be reminded
that my current situation
is not my final destination.

There's more to my life
beyond the fog of today.

Rescue me
from the anxiousness I feel
at the impermanence
of all things.

Quell in me
the anger I feel
at the relentless
passage of time.

I grasp
at the hands
of the clock.
I wear myself out.

Rescue me
from my attachment to
sentimentality
and nostalgia.

Teach me
to open my hands
and receive
yesterday as a gift.

Cellularly,
I am a whole different person
in seven years
and that's involuntary.

Intentionally,
what would I wish myself
to become
in seven years?

Resilient?
Kind?
Grateful?
Hopeful?

May I see this Low
as the deeper part of me
volunteering for
that transformation.

I do not get back
what has gone away
and I cannot become again
who I was.

Help me let go of what was.
My attachment to yesterday
distracts me
from the day I'm in.

I want to wrap my arms
around gifts Today offers
and learn myself,
as I am now.

May the sweetness
I find in this day
lead to hopeful expectation
for what comes next.

Remind me
that the pursuit of fairness
can trap me
in the loop of analysis.

Remind me that the question
I get to ask about yesterday
is what to do with what it gave me
now that I've been given today.

May thankfulness
for the gift of existence
teach me to be generous
with the way I hold my memories.

Just beneath my heart,
weighing like a stone
against my stomach,
is the nausea of absence.

I miss the way things were.
I miss the way I used to be.
This is not what I thought would happen.
I am not who I thought I'd be.

Show me
that these thoughts and feelings
are only doorways to more fulfilling and energizing
thoughts and feelings.

May the depth of my sadness
at what I no longer have
forge an attentive thankfulness in me
to what exists and to what might yet exist.

Help me loosen my grip
on the phantom of yesterday
that I might welcome each new day
with appreciation and awe.

ppy

Today,
may it be enough
to believe
one day
I will experience
a height of joy
that matches
the depth
of this pain.

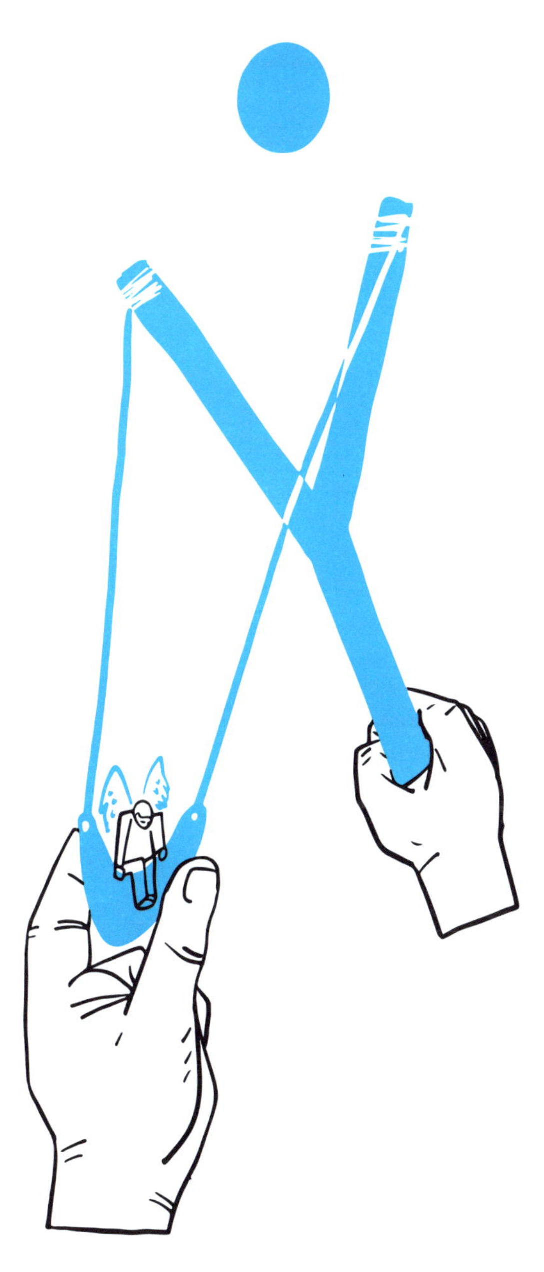

If this is described as heavy,
it means there is an opposite
known as light.

If this is described as dark,
it means there is an opposite
known as bright.

If this is described as Low,
it means there is an opposite
known as high.

I know this to be true
because I have experienced both,
even though right now
in the Low
the opposite
feels like a distant memory.

May I remember the opposites today:
There will be a tomorrow, in the highs,
where I remember this present Low.

I can imagine
feeling peace and clarity
but only in the way
I can imagine tomorrow morning.

It is just out of reach.
It is a maybe.

Help me recognize
this feeling as Hope.
Lift my eyes from their myopic stare
at the blank space where certainty used to be.

There's a voyage in me.
An adventure
I froze
within my imagination.

It is a journey
too terrifying to consider
and too wonderful to make real.

I'd rather preserve it in possibility,
drift in quiet desperation
and gamble iceberging another's dispatch

than thaw
to the invitation
that I am worthy of
the odyssey
of loving my life.

I want to love my life again.

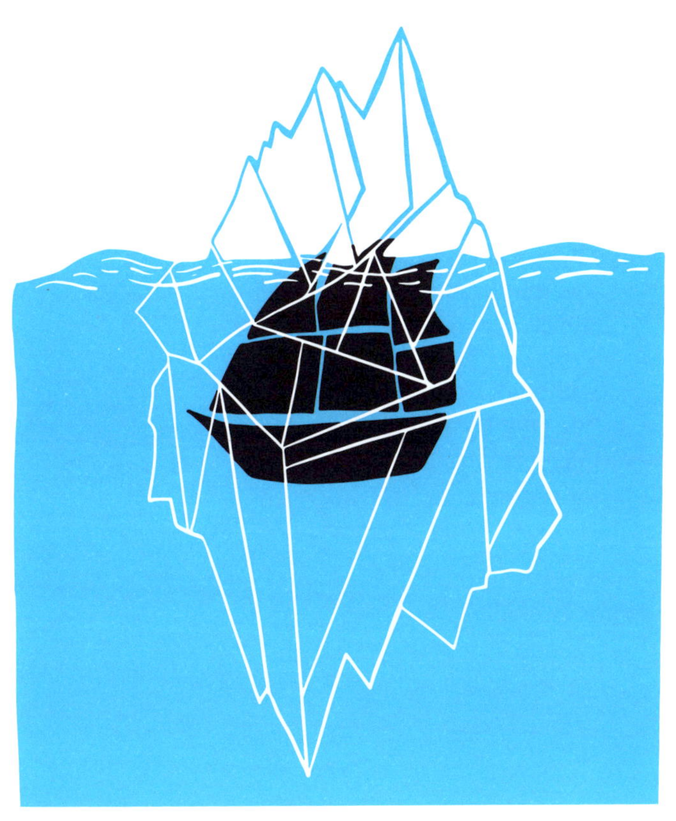

I do not need an immediate cure.
I need to believe
that wholeness and wellness
and clarity and peace are possible.

Grant me
not a momentary glimpse
but an enduring vision
for newness.

I once felt so lost,
lost at sea.

Then I was found again.

When you've been found,
you realize
you were never really lost.
You were just on a journey
to a place
you've never been to.

Today,
may you see
that you are on a journey
to a place
you've never been to.

It's okay not to have a plan
on the days you can't clearly see.
And especially
when you can't clearly see yourself.

Go on a long walk.
Avoid the internet.
Eat some nachos.
Notice bugs.
Listen to the birdsong in your neighborhood.
Be around those who love you.

Vision is rooted
in ingredients
such as these.

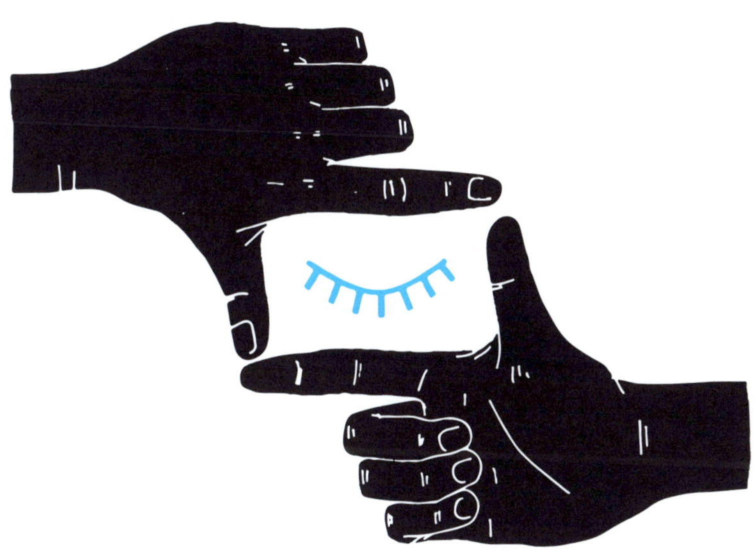

Depression is
seeing the truth
about everything
while
believing the lie
that this definition of truth
is all that there is.

May I be reminded
that the truth in this Low
is not all that there is.

May the Truth set me free.

Our prayers, pills
and practices
are wrapped together
in our bodies.

May each
do its good work
to bring about
Wholeness in us.

10,000
S
T
W
T
F
S

You are not your breakdown.
You are not your fire.
You are not even the vehicle
forced to a complete stop.

You are the very road trip
on which all kinds of fantastical experiences take place.

One day, you will treasure them all.

Grant me eyes to see
not so much past my fear
but to see my fear in the landscape
of my fruitful and expansive life.

Teach me to look back
and see my own past.
You brought me here.
You'll take me there.

Teach me
to look back
at the myriad of doorways
I've passed through

and know that I am here
after having trusted You
to lead me
through those doors.

I am here
in this good place
because I followed You
through those doors.

Today
may I remember
storms
eventually
end.

Rescue me
from the stranglehold
certainty has
on me.

I don't want to "know"
in the way I have known.
Being sure
has let me down.

Teach me to let go.
Teach me the pace
that comes from learning.
Teach me to trust and to hope.

Doubtlessness has led
to disillusionment
and that disillusionment
has led to suffering.

I would rather hope
because hope produces dreams
and dreams
make me feel alive.

May this suffering
produce perseverance
and may that perseverance
develop character in me.

May the character in me
dare to hope
so that I might dream again
and feel alive.

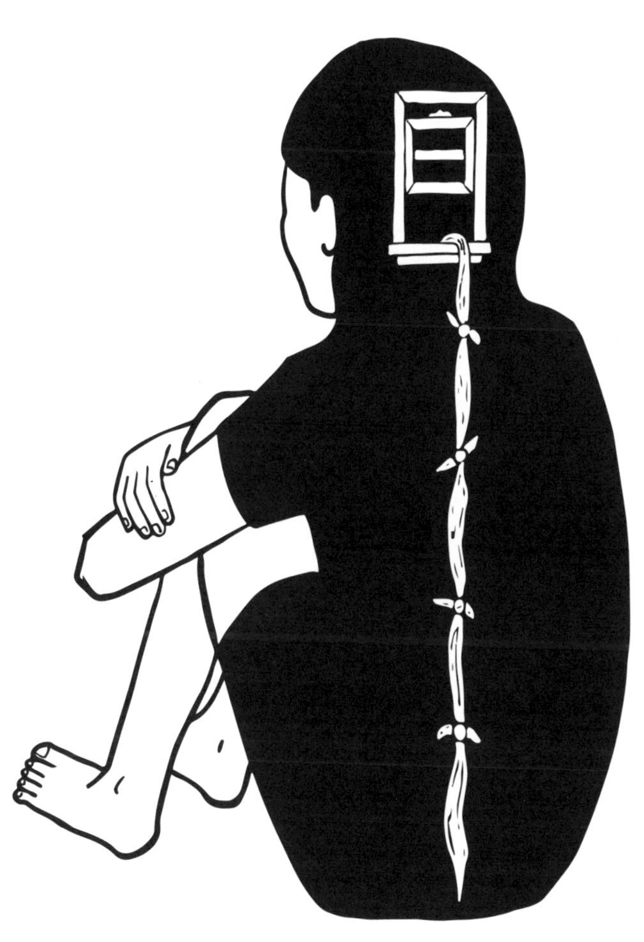

The remedy
for unrealized hope
is sadness.

Sadness cleanses my soul
of the expectation
that things should work out as I wish.

On the other side
of that valley
is new hope.

May my eyes adjust
in the darkness
of the valley

so that I might see
the dim light
that has been available
all along.

May the fear I feel
on the threshold of the unknown
give way to the nervousness
of anticipation.

Tomorrow
is not a conclusion.
Tomorrow
is an invitation.

Teach me to see
the emptiness of unknowing
as an open hand
and an offering.

Teach me to see
the darkness of the inconclusive
as a question
I get to answer.

When I look back
at my life,
what will stand out
will be all the
unexpected growth
from moments
in which I thought
it was all over.

May I apply
that future wisdom
to this moment
in which I feel like
it's all over.

Minds have their own weather system.
Tornadoes and hurricanes
eventually run out of energy.

May I remember this too:
This Low
shall pass.

I am worn out
by the chase
after what
is lacking.

Teach me
to receive "this"
instead of
wanting "that."

Teach me
to be "here"
instead of wishing
I was "there."

I worry and fret
that I am behind
that I am "not there yet"
that I am running out of time.

Remind me
that my destination
is not a place or an accomplishment.
My destination is peace and wholeness.

Please stay.

At least for today.

You don't need to
figure it all out,
accomplish anything great,
be acclaimed,
know all the stuff,
be on the cutting edge
of whatever frontier
you think you need to be on
to make it in this world.

Just stay with this:
the promise
of your incarnation.

Please.
I promise you . . .

There are roads ahead
you have never imagined
traveling.
And there will be a moment
in the not too far future
in which you'll look back at
this moment
and be grateful
you stayed with it.

You'll be glad you stayed
with the promise
that you don't actually know
what's going to happen next
and you'll have grossly
underestimated
the surprises Providence
has hidden along the way.

This is the promise
of your incarnation.
And I promise
it'll be worth it.

So
please stay.
At least for today.

## Before You Go, Please Stay

988 is the Suicide and Crisis Lifeline. It was launched on January 1, 2005, by the Substance Abuse and Mental Health Services Administration (SAMHSA) and can receive as many as 500,000 calls, texts, and messages every month.[12] If you google "988," you're not only greeted by text, call, and web portals, you're also offered prewritten messages you can use to start a conversation with someone.

Messages like,

"I don't want to die, but I don't know how to live. Talking with you may help me feel safe. Are you free to talk?"

And

"This is really hard for me to say, but I'm having painful thoughts and it might help to talk. Are you free?"

Someone is always there.

Always.

The very first suicide support line was started in the early 1950s by an Anglican priest named Edward Chad Varah. As the rector of a church in London, he learned that up to three Londoners sought to end their lives every day, and dedicated a phone line at his church to anyone in emotional distress. I think it's worth noting that the phone from which he ran the initial helpline was located in the church's crypt. Let's give the man points for being both empathetic and poetic.

Rector Varah's relationship with suicide didn't begin when he got to London, though. Twenty years earlier, he had been graveside at a funeral for a fourteen-year-old girl who thought she'd contracted an STI. She hadn't. She was simply menstruating. But because she didn't understand what was happening with her body, she felt like she was broken and chose to end her life.[13]

That's the moment of Varah's story I find most compelling and the one this book's heart most deeply resonates with. That young girl was experiencing something natural to her fourteen-year-old body. But because she lacked connections to better information and persons with whom she could trust her complex human journey, she believed there was something terribly wrong. So it is with far too many of us. We might be having mental and emotional experiences that are entirely appropriate but, in the absence of the connections that keep us Whole, we end up categorizing those experiences as "brokenness" and labeling them with shame.

We might find ourselves listless instead of fulfilled by the work of our hands.
We might find ourselves feeling lonely.
We might find ourselves confused about what matters.
We might find ourselves hung up on the past.
We might find ourselves hungrily clamoring for the attention of others.
We might find ourselves feeling robotic and mechanized.
We might find ourselves fearful of tomorrow.

We might find ourselves feeling a lot like that fourteen-year-old girl having her first period and wondering *Is it okay that I am this way?* Yes, Beloved. It is okay. You are okay. Even if you're not okay right now. Being in the Low is part of being alive.

We pray because we're human, not because we're religious. And we spend time in the Low for the very same reason. For many of us, the question isn't whether or not we will enter into depression but how to be there when we do. And while Scott and I can't answer that question for you, specifically, we can confidently tell you that you will not be there alone.

Consider this book a little bit like dialing 988. It'll always be here. And anytime you open it up, you'll be greeted with words and images you can use if you want some help reconnecting with God, your loved ones, or even your own soul while being in the Low.

# Notes

1. Previously published in Justin McRoberts and Scott Erickson, *Prayer: Forty Days of Practice* (New York: Waterbrook, 2019).
2. Johann Hari, *Lost Connections: Uncovering the Real Causes of Depression—and the Unexpected Solutions* (New York: Bloomsbury, 2018).
3. Many thanks to Contemplative Outreach for their generous permission in allowing us to use this prayer in our book. We'd suggest you look deeper into Welcoming Prayer as Contemplative Outreach teaches it by visiting www.contemplativeoutreach.org/welcoming-prayer-method/.
4. "What Does This Life Really Mean?—Jim Carrey," YouTube video, 5:44, posted by Absolute Motivation on November 4, 2017, https://youtube.com/wTblbYqQQag?si=U9-ohqNpyxWB5rnz.
5. Riccardo Tamburini, "World Poverty Statistics 2024," Social Income, accessed September 30, 2024, https://socialincome.org/en/int/world-poverty-statistics-2024.
6. "Global Nuclear Weapons Spending Surges to $91.4 Billion," ICAN, June 17, 2024, https://www.icanw.org/global_nuclear_weapons_spending_surges_to_91_4_billion.
7. "2023 Holiday to Reach Record Spending Levels," National Retail Federation, November 2, 2023, https://nrf.com/media-center/press-releases/2023-holiday-reach-record-spending-levels.
8. J. Michael Straczynski and Ron Garney, *The Amazing Spider-Man* #537 (1999), 16.
9. "2000: The Sydney Vault Debacle and the Apparatus Norms Hypothesis," Gymnastics History, May 21, 2022, https://www.gymnastics-history.com/2022/05/2000-the-sydney-vault-debacle-and-the-apparatus-norms-hypothesis/.
10. Dan Witters, "U.S. Depression Rates Reach New Highs," Gallup, May 17, 2023, https://news.gallup.com/poll/505745/depression-rates-reach-new-highs.
11. Romans 7:15.
12. SAMHSA, "Lifeline Timeline" 988 Suicide & Crisis Lifeline, accessed September 30, 2024, https://www.samhsa.gov/find-help/988/lifeline-timeline.
13. "Our History," The Samaritans of Rhode Island, accessed September 30, 2024, http://www.samaritansri.org/who-we-are/our-history.

# Gratitudes

## Justin thanks

Scott for the years of partnership and conversation (and for the Thai chicken meal that one time). • Baker Books for letting us make this book. • Stephanie Duncan Smith and Grace P. Cho for the editing help. • Joy Eggerich Reed for helping me navigate the book world. • The CCO and Jubilee Conference for forming the McErickson connection. • Rooted Coffee and States Coffee (where I wrote most of my part) • Asa, Katelyn, Amy, Mom, and Mo • The Good Way • Anam Cara Ministries • Frank Tate • Dan Portnoy

## Scott thanks

Justin for inviting me to become an author with him oh so many years ago and for telling me to keep working out my content in front of an audience. • Baker Books for making this magic real. • Stephanie Duncan Smith and Grace P. Cho . . . this is starting to sound redundant. • Holly, Anders, Elsa, Jones • Kurt and Royal for last-minute edits in the studio. • Joy Eggerich Reed • Cynthia Hernandez • Angie and Mike Leone for the perfect place to finish the imagery. • The color Blue

# About the Authors

**Justin McRoberts** is an author, coach, and retreat leader who has also done a bit of music in the past. This is his eighth book and his third with Scott. He lives in Martinez, California, and he calls his mom every day.

**CONNECT WITH JUSTIN**

JustinMcRoberts.com

**Scott Erickson** is an artist, author, performance speaker, and creative curate who mixes autobiography, mythology, and aesthetics to create art and moments that speak to our deepest experiences. This is his fifth book and third with Justin, but who's counting? He lives in Vancouver, Washington, with his wife and three kids.

**CONNECT WITH SCOTT**

ScottEricksonArt.com

Thank you for spending time with us *In the Low*. If you believe people you care about might find help here, we've made it easier for you to buy a box of them to give out.

Visit us at **InTheLow.com**